Hélène Giannecchini

Alix Cléo Roubaud:
a portrait in fragments

Translated by Thea Petrou

SYLPH
EDITIONS

UNE IMAGE
PEUT-ÊTRE
VRAIE.
ALIX CLÉO ROUBAUD

First published in 2014
by Éditions du Seuil

ALIX CLÉO ROUBAUD:
A PORTRAIT IN FRAGMENTS

Contents

Intentions · 9
Earliest Records · 17
The Brother · 27
Darkroom · 35
Bookshelves · 43
Ludwig Wittgenstein · 51
Jean Eustache · 55
Bearing Witness · 71
They said · 79
Doubling, Shifting, Repeating · 81
Lifting Belly · 87
Embodiments · 89
Breathing · 107
Si quelque chose noir · 121
The Institution · 137
The Thing That's Missing · 145
Le Baiser · 151
(BLACK) · 159

Coda
    JACQUES ROUBAUD: Afterword · 163
    THEA PETROU: Chère Hélène… · 173

List of Photographs and Illustrations · 181
Endnotes · 185
Alix's Cléo Roubaud's Works · 186
Note to the Reader · 187
Acknowledgements · 188
About the Author · 189

Translator's
Note to Reader

Alix Cléo Roubaud's often unusual punctuation and irregular spacing between words – particularities of her journal entries that were originally written using a typewriter – have been respected.

References to Alix's artworks have been kept in the original French throughout the text. On page 186 a list of works gives the titles both in French and English.

Intentions

ALIX CLÉO ROUBAUD was born on 19 January 1952 in Mexico. She died on 28 January 1983, in rue des Francs-Bourgeois in Paris, a few days after her 31st birthday. She was the first child of Marcelle and Arthur Edward Blanchette. Her brother Marc was born in 1957 in Pretoria, South Africa. The daughter of a diplomat, her childhood was governed by trips and regular upheavals dictated by the posting of her father first to Mexico, then to Egypt, Portugal and Greece. This well-to-do but nomadic way of life led her to correspond for long periods with friends and loved ones she'd had to leave behind. Today I have around 800 letters, notes and telegrams of which around a third were written by her. This book is nourished by these documents.

In 1967, Alix Cléo Roubaud enrolled at the University of Ottawa, aged 15, to study, somewhat haphazardly, psychology, literature and architecture, before settling on philosophy. She also attended a few classes in Chinese and journalism at Carleton University. In 1972, wishing to live away from her family, the young Alix left Canada to pursue philosophy studies in Aix-en-Provence. This choice was also motivated by health reasons: the Mediterranean climate helped in the treatment of her asthma, which had caused her suffering since childhood and was worsening with time. Three years later, in 1975, she set off for Paris and enrolled in the department of Freudian studies at the University of Paris VIII. At the age of 24, she began a doctoral thesis under the supervision of Jacques Bouveresse. Her subject was 'Wittgenstein: Style and Thought – Remarks on Philosophical Writing'. She never finished her research.

In 1977, she met W. and they had a passionate and turbulent love affair. The young man of German origin studied architecture. In an envelope found in Alix's apartment, I discovered letters and notes exchanged by the two lovers. Tender notes left for the other person while they were still sleeping gave way to letters full of contempt and insults. W. and Alix also seem to have shared a lot: she studied German – her exercise books of vocabulary and grammar are testament to this – and deciphered Wittgenstein in the original language; they took photographs together. Some of the most morbid photos were taken after Alix had ingested a fatal dose of sleeping tablets, just before the emergency services arrived. During an interview in 2010, he told me that she had chosen the subject matter. These images taken from the brink of death are not part of the Alix Cléo Roubaud collection. I have only seen them once, briefly. W. kept hold of them.

In Paris, her emotional and social life became more intense. From 1979, she held a monthly social event in her Paris apartment on rue Vieille-du-Temple. These lively, alcohol-fuelled soirées were an opportunity to meet intellectuals, to show some of her photographic works in progress, and sometimes even to sell them.

In 1978, references to La Bourboule began to appear in letters to her mother: a thermal spa hotel in Puy-de-Dôme where she stayed on a number of occasions to treat her asthma. She took some photographs in this quaint, peaceful place. La Bourboule became a yearly treatment for Alix Cléo Roubaud, whose respiratory illness was her main concern.

On 29 June 1979, she met the director Jean Eustache. They immediately entered into an affair and telephoned each other regularly. On 5 July 1980, she filmed *Les Photos d'Alix* with him and his son. To introduce this short film to students, Alix Cléo wrote a textual manifesto, a misappropriation of Ludwig Wittgenstein's *Tractatus logico-philosophicus*, which proved the theoretical calibre of her research as much as her sense of humour. *Les Photos d'Alix* won a César for best short fiction film in 1982, a few months after Eustache committed suicide on 5 November 1981. Deeply affected by this loss, she left to spend some time alone in the south of France and, just a month after Eustache's death, she wrote what would be the final version of her will.

In December 1979, Alix Cléo met Jacques Roubaud, whom she described as an unassuming, even austere mathematician with 'Victorian charm'. She fell in love with him. From March to June, they travelled to Amiens, Fès (Morocco), Avignon and Cambridge, where they got married on 11 June 1980. A few days later they held a big party in Paris to celebrate their marriage with their loved ones. Georges Perec wrote an epithalamium for them:

> Alix-Cléo is married to Jacques
> and Jacques is married to Alix-Cléo
> This is a joyful coincidence and so today
> they are both allied and bound together [...].[1]

From 1979, her photography work became more focused: her relationship with her poet-husband, their collaborative projects and shared reading, undoubtedly influenced her output. Around this time the main themes of her explorations in photography emerged: conceptualization of the image, self-portraiture, doubling, repetition and death. Despite this positive influence and the joy of newly married life, Alix was still subject to violent bouts of depression. Fatigue, anxiety and suicide attempts were often mentioned in her private journal, in letters, or by those who knew her. On 14 August 1980, she tried again to end her life at Jacques Roubaud's family home in Saint-Félix, near Carcassonne. A few days later, in the workshop belonging to her brother-in-law, Pierre

Getzler, adjacent to the main house, she created her most famous photography series: *Si quelque chose noir*.

In January 1982, after a trip to Tunis with Jacques Roubaud, Alix Cléo took part in a big group exhibition at the Maison des arts de Créteil, called *Une autre photographie (Another Photography)*. That same year she was chosen by Alain Desvergnes to participate in the Rencontres photographiques d'Arles, which would take place six months after her death.

On 28 January 1983, early in the morning, she was found dead by her husband at their marital home in Paris.

In 1984, Jacques Roubaud decided to publish her private journal, with the help of Denis Roche. He selected for publication only the notebooks filled during the time of their relationship (1979-1983), and he redacted the passages deemed most private. He inserted photographs by Alix Cléo Roubaud into the volume.

Until 2009, Alix Cléo Roubaud's work had been almost entirely forgotten. Jacques Roubaud was in possession of the 660 photographs left in a jumble after her death. Today these images form part of the prestigious collections held by the Bibliothèque nationale de France, the Centre Georges-Pompidou, the Maison européenne de la photographie, the Bibliothèque municipale de Lyon, the Musée des beaux-arts de Montréal and the Institut Mémoires de l'édition contemporaine (IMEC).

THIS IS A POSSIBLE timeline of her life. But I find purely biographical writing difficult. From classifying her letters, finding official documents, and compiling an inventory of her photographs, I have established a table of six columns: day, month, year, event, place, people involved. But this succession of events is far from exhaustive: I have practically no information about the first 25 years of her life, and the most detailed period (1979-1983) is essentially filled in by her husband. The annals of a life, often partial or incomplete, call for invention: you must plug the gaps, link up the facts between them, mould flesh around the skeleton of dates. If you set yourself the task of reconstructing an existence, you should do it through feeling: relive the impulses of the protagonist, detail her affections. I should talk about Alix Cléo's love for Jacques Roubaud, her attraction to Eustache, her resentment towards her mother. Sticking to the facts is never enough; I would also have to weave an account from the thoughts that I have been able to gather, guess at some of her reactions, now disappeared without trace. But this intimacy with a subject can be dangerous: I don't trust the sense of identification which arises from close proximity. I don't want to speak for Alix Cléo Roubaud. Of her hopes and attachments, I only know what she has written, I will not fantasize about the rest. Fiction thwarts the scrupulous objectivity of the archive.

To begin the work, I wanted to know Alix Cléo Roubaud and I got completely lost in the search for details: what clothes did she wear, who were her friends, what became of this guy Bill with whom she had an affair in Ottawa? But does it all matter? In the attempt to accumulate traces, the subject is buried, and you manage to render the insignificant crucial. I don't like this sort of retrospective reading; it is a little too easy to work with the dead.

Any writing that describes a life bends before it. The writing must fade before the story because it is not the writing that matters but rather this other to whom you owe a certain loyalty, a respect for their memory. It is impossible to recount everything; for a biography, I would have to be selective. I don't want to choose what is worthy of interest here. I refuse that power.

Alix Cléo Roubaud will never appear through all the proof gathered round her. The hours of interviews I have conducted with the ghosts of her journal, the letters written to her mother, her will: I have mere fragments of light, but her heart remains opaque. And that shadow grows, heavy with everyone's constructions of her. They have described her to me one by one: 'incredibly cultivated', 'Jacques Roubaud's partner in crime', 'debauched and ruthlessly ambitious', 'great photographer' then 'at a loose end and lacking in talent', 'seriously asthmatic', 'slightly ill', 'incredibly cheerful', 'terribly suicidal', the list goes on. So many points of view to make sense of, only to conclude that I am not interested in that. I no longer want to untangle the facts from the stories because that undertaking seems futile. I content myself with collecting the pieces of a mosaic and composing my own image, with or without them.

I CANNOT RECOUNT the life of Alix Cléo Roubaud, but I am able to present her archive and her photography. I walk a razor edge between the dates, the events that might bring elements of understanding, and my resistance to genetic analysis and biographical research. Not only is the life not the work, but too many stories tend to cloud our view. The *Journal*, revealing only those fragments written between 1979 and 1983, is the main document of Alix Cléo's that has been published. Often thought to be her only piece of writing, it eclipses a whole other side of her work. The theoretical writings and the letters make up a great deal of her literary output that deserves consideration, and they introduce a variety of tones and registers. Despite containing dense, robust passages on photography, the *Journal* is often dominated by her intimate thoughts and sorrows. Then there are the photographs, in which we try to recognize the things we have read. Recognition brings a certain pleasure, but it is not seeing.

To delve into the archive is to accept a fragmented view. I thought I was setting off to meet Alix Cléo Roubaud, but the meeting never happened. I could say, sentimentally, that she evades every attempt to pin her down, but the truth is that she no longer exists. The inexorable nature of death drives us to interpretation in an attempt to fix in place that which, in reality, has no clear outline. The silence of the deceased can never challenge exegesis.

To avoid this trap, when the traces are confused or missing entirely, I prefer to use 'I'. Through modesty, through honesty, I choose to assert my own subjectivity, like a vow of ignorance, a barrier against the temptation to declare 'she was this or that'. I make do with my view and the freedom that it entails; I can, if I so choose, break up the chronology, scatter ellipses all through my narrative. Protected by the first-person singular, I assert nothing; I merely suggest. And just as Alix appeared to me in fragments, letters, images, and through reconstructed accounts, so too I wish to write.

I began my work on Alix Cléo Roubaud at the start of 2008. It was on reading *Quelque chose noir*,* the volume of elegiac poetry dedicated to her by Jacques Roubaud, that I wanted to fill in the interstices where I thought I imagined her. I realized, after getting caught up in her life and her work, that the interest of the archive does not lie so much in the result itself as in the approach: complete immersion in a life which is not mine, carrying out an investigation with no resolution.

IF THE ARCHIVE fervently accumulates, classifies and inventories all the traces of the past, the valuation of a work, on the contrary, calls for them to be relinquished. Institutions exhibit the quintessence of creation. Rushed notes, overexposed photographs and poor drawings have no place in a museum. I appreciate this selectiveness: there is nothing worse than those average reconstructions that seek to temper virtuosity with the everyday.

Yet I am drawn to those residues that prove the universal triviality of the greatest artists. The failed takes reconstitute a process, remind us that every work is a making, a tentative movement forward achieved by trial and error. And it is also the banal, the traces that do not make much impact, the space around the art-

---

* *Translator's note*: *Quelque chose noir* has been translated into English. See Rosmarie Waldrop, *Some Thing Black* (Elmwood Park: Dalkey Archive Press, 1990).

work that I want to talk about. I see no need to omit this clamour of failed attempts and crossings-out, of stubborn, lingering voices; those people who welcomed me and handed over their memories; the disappointment of certain archives. If the institution presents us with the final, polished work of art, I want to make space for the rough workings of the archive.

Earliest Records

Alix Cléo Roubaud on a beach in Greece in May 1967.
On the back she has written: 'My favourite photo, a symbol
of [...] the *joie de vivre* and *carpe diem* that I dream of [...].'
(Part of the handwriting is illegible, the image must have
been ripped out of an album.)

THE FIRST SET OF DOCUMENTS in the Alix Cléo Roubaud collection dates from 23 July 1966, at 49 Samara Road in Athens, and ends in rue Henri-Fabre in Aix, in 1973. From the age of 14 to 21, Alix kept up a correspondence with a friend, Sylvie, whom she had met at the Institut français in Athens. She told her about what she had been reading, her discovery of philosophy, of sexuality, and her first sources of anguish. This starting point of the archive, chronologically speaking, turned up several years after I had begun my research. One evening in 2011, Sylvie went to a bookshop where Jacques Roubaud was reading, gave him a big orange ring-binder, and left after mumbling a few words. He didn't ask for her surname, and he gave me the file without opening it. Until 2013, I didn't know who Sylvie was, or if she was still alive – the letters were enough for me.

FOR A LONG TIME, I didn't know what to make of this object in my library. Outdated, conspicuous, its bright orange cover looked out of place among the other binders of Alix's documents, sorted according to a strict colour code of dark blue, black and grey. The archive is built on this work in the tangible – sorting, listing, classifying – and this folder was the only thing I had left just as it had been given to me. Sylvie had gone to the trouble of putting the letters in plastic wallets, in date order of when they were sent, so I hadn't physically gone through these documents myself. The contents of the file revealed an Alix Cléo Roubaud who was unfamiliar to me, not the person I was writing about. This quite unremarkable correspondence harboured a story which seemed impossible to me, a biographical reading that I refused to give in to.

And yet.

In 1966, the Blanchette family was in Athens, where Arthur, the diplomat father, had been named chargé d'affaires. The mother, Marcelle, the younger brother, Marc, and Alix accompanied him. They had a privileged lifestyle: they lived in a splendid villa in the suburbs of Athens (a former friend, impressed by the residence, still remembers the 'rave' she held there), Alix was enrolled at the Institut français, where she was surrounded by the children of diplomats and businessmen, and she had a car and driver at her disposal. She was there during the military coup of 1967, though she experienced it from a distance. The colonels' dictatorship, which began in Athens on the night of 21 April, worried her, even though it didn't affect her directly. In a newspaper image from period, shot from a balcony, a tank is shown crossing a road of the Greek capital. The tank imposes its menacing horizontality, cannon and outward-pointing submachine guns, on the verticality of the street, and passers-by are gripped by the spectacle. This too was the environment that Alix grew up in. Next to the photograph of an adolescent of 15 years, smiling on an idyllic beach, there is this one of the army marching on the city. The *carpe diem* spirit that Alix Cléo dreamed of was now impossible. Her childhood was not spent wrapped up in herself, in blissful naivety, but exposed to the outside world, cast into its brutality and contradictions. The diplomatic cocoon that she grew up in existed in a specific environment, was a consequence of it, and she knew that only too well.

Alix grew up in a shifting, wealthy and political world where her father's posts and the different countries she passed through shaped her outlook. In Eustache's film *Les Photos d'Alix* (1980), she describes a picture of a man standing in a field which belongs to him, and she says: 'That's something I've always really envied, people who have their own piece of land, a home, somewhere they belong. I've never had that.' Born in Mexico, Alix moved to Canada, her home country, for the first time at the age of seven, after having lived in Egypt during the Suez Canal crisis in 1956, and in South Africa, where her brother was born. After five years in Ottawa, the Blanchette family again left for Greece. The final return home to Canada did not happen until 1968, and it came as a relief. In her letters to Sylvie, Alix describes her happiness at being back among familiar landscapes, the North American forest, and its organ-pipe trees.

> I'm writing you this at the end of February, a time when an extraordinary softness spreads through our snowy country (the ice is melting, and the sun turning warm again above the clouds).

But her family identity was no less complex there. Francophone without being from Quebec, the Blanchette family were part of a historical and linguistic minority in Ontario. They lived a few kilometres from Montreal, near the river separating the two states, on the boundary. The space between was a recurring motif for Alix Cléo: as a child, she was not a citizen of the countries she lived in, she spoke English and French fluently; as an adult, she left Canada for France, but refused to change her nationality.

When she married Jacques Roubaud, she had to face a maze of officialdom that reminded her of her foreign status. She described this punishment humorously in a letter to her mother in March 1980:

> I will find out in roughly a month's time when we will be able to get married. The commission is investigating me (as they do every foreigner in the same situation); I have to prove that I'm not trying to evade Canadian justice, that I'm not a bigamist, or rather biandrous, etc. that I'm marrying for Love. So, I'm making googly, love-struck eyes from one office to the next, from the prefecture to the subprefecture.

Being the daughter of a diplomat shaped Alix Cléo Roubaud, even if only from a social standpoint. Some of her close friends remember her 'embassy French', her taste and flair for society events. She certainly developed a surprising intelligence and ease very early on. 'When I was two,I ate only cornflakes.very precocious,aged three,I spoke French,Dialectal Arabic,English,' she noted in January 1983 after a trip to Tunis, where her father was appointed ambassador. The brilliance of her letters to Sylvie is striking, her mastery of language admirable. She was only 14 years old, and she spoke of 'phonetic whistling', 'a delightful egotist', of Descartes and Saint Augustine. Alix read a great deal and had a passionate interest in philosophers and poets. One of her classmates remembers her first French essay. The teacher didn't believe Alix had written it at first. After she read it out to the class, everyone was astonished by the quality of her writing and her wit. 'She was already well ahead of the rest,' he told me.

Sylvie and Alix also sent each other drawings and photographs. Epistolary writing is a practice that involves distance, absence, and it is only through image that transformations are noticed. This is how Alix was able to see the time that stood between them and their childhood, the evidence of their separation.

> A photo. You have grown old. Cheekbones, eyes and mouth are surer. Have you grown taller? I think you're beautiful... And faced with an image on a piece of paper, my eyes falter, stubbornly persist, try desperately to come to terms with the mobile reality that it represents. Weary of this futile effort, I tuck the photo away into my purse, unsatisfied.[2]

The image holds within it a lack, the snapshot, the momentary, bears witness to the passing of time and the impossible presence of the photograph's subject. In the photograph, physical change is no longer a process, but an event, the image an inconsistency.

In 1980, Alix Cléo Roubaud wrote that the time of the photograph was the future anterior, a paradoxical, melancholic conjugation indicating that which, in the future, is already finished, the 'that will have been'. It is the future past, the instant the shot is taken. In Alix's words: 'when you see this, it will no longer be'. This instant in the present which you see through the viewfinder, the moment you want to hold onto, is gone the moment your finger pushes down on the shutter release. The latent image will be discovered once it has been exposed on paper. The scene is consumed rather than seen. The letter seems to be exposed to the same clash of temporalities, recounting a present that will have slipped away by the time of reading, and so, we might rewrite Alix's words as: 'when you read this, it will no longer be'. And the reader who deciphers the letters to Sylvie decades later cannot help but notice the irrevocable distance of the episodes narrated and her own inability to make them reappear.

THESE LETTERS are not central to my approach. The situations evoked in them are unfamiliar to me and I don't know the people mentioned. I have not thought about trying to find them. It is Alix the adult, photographer and writer that I am interested in. This piece of the archive, however, is moving; it reveals a child Alix, creates a time before 1979 and, by giving an insight into her background, brings her closer. I must avoid falling into the trap of relying on biographical detail, without completely setting aside the accounts given. This document must help to understand, not to explain. It informs us about the first years of Alix's life in the same way we ask our friends or parents, 'who were you before, what story led you to me?' I don't expect it to yield the seeds of the work to come. The letters to Sylvie are not a liminal space leading to the artist Alix Cléo Roubaud, the life and the work are never perfectly aligned. Those with whom Alix spoke about her childhood have passed on snippets of their memories to me. After she died, they looked back to her early years in search of the source of her melancholy: death often needs reasons, mourning takes place supported by the reasons why. I don't need to account for her depression just to speak about her.

Anecdotes abound when I question those who knew Alix Cléo Roubaud. Memory reconstructs, words weave stories around the pictures left behind. Some memories are collective and so have been recounted to me many times. Recognizing the pattern, I listen with interest to the variations and, when I compare these accounts, I note the changes in perspective, the discrepancies in dates or settings. The fluctuations in perception lead to all sorts of truths, like different facets of a single object. The scene is never exactly the same, like in theatre, where every rehearsal introduces a tiny modification, shaping the final event.

I recognized in the letters to Sylvie what some people had been describing as the seminal event, the trigger. They had been accounting for Alix's fragility with a precise incident from her adolescence. After hearing versions of the story related by those close to her, I was able to read Alix's account. I never thought I'd be able to get close to the original episode after following the detour of the other narratives.

Saturday 6 January 1968
I wrote the last letter you received from me during the night: my mother's crisis had erupted a few hours earlier; in my bedroom she gave vent to her rage, her fears, her mistrust, her contempt; she spoke rapidly, loudly, infuriated, while I quietly stumbled – as quietly as I could – through every sentence. I have a Dantesque memory of that hour; it felt like Martine was being shot in front of me, in the very calm of my room, shot down with accusations: Martine the pervert, Martine the Machiavellian, Martine seduced a silly young girl with her trickery, Martine the criminal, Martine the pervert, Martine the pervert, Martine the pervert... The gunshots kept coming at an unrelenting and calculated pace, I defended myself with calm words which endeavoured to explain the situation clearly and reasonably. She left in a fury, and I realized wearily that I hated her from the bottom of my heart, without violence, just a gnawing, unforgiving hatred; because I had loved her, my mother, I hated her; because I had loved her, I should no longer see Martine: I was trembling with hatred towards this being who, through the love I had for her, had been capable of flooding the pure, light world

I'd known with Martine with a torrent of dirt, filth, sin, nauseating sordidness. The tyranny of love. [...]

The next day I was calling Martine. It was so absurd, nothing was finished. I was slightly reassured: it all depended on my own will. I was no longer subject to a superior play of influences. I thought I was Sartrean, I savoured Gide's *The Fruits of the Earth*: it was time to understand that philosophy was something that only had value in action. I was of the age where I had to begin to decide the course of my own life according to my own freedom of choice. Gone were the emotions of the day before.

Since Martine and I loved each other, I would see her, I would love her, I had the courage of my convictions. I didn't have the right to hurt my mother; for her, officially, I had broken off the affair, I was no longer seeing her; I would avoid any scandal; it came down to a question of caution.

At the age of 15, Alix had an affair with Martine, a woman of about 30. She often took refuge with her companion, experienced the rapture of long conversations, a new sexuality. When her mother, Marcelle Blanchette, found out, she demanded that the relationship be ended, citing corruption of a minor and social conventions. Alix then decided to continue the affair in secret. But her mother, who seemed to be reading her letters and her private journal, uncovered her daughter's deceit a few months later.

October 1968
'Only in winter do the pine and cypress show they are evergreen' – a Chinese proverb. It is true that philosophy consoles, I said to myself, flicking through the dictionary of proverbs; then I turned to Boisdeffre: 'Adolescence is a

great man-eater.' Then, Camus. Make no mistake about it and don't brush it off as a contemptible sign of intellectual dilettantism: it is true that philosophy consoles. Absurdity confronted with the absurd; the solidarity of those who have been through it is precious to me. It is all I have left. They have taken away my reason for living; they found out about my secret affair from a letter I was writing, which I inadvertently left out in the open on my desk; they humiliated me, slapped me, grounded me; the fragile structure of lies collapsed like a house of cards, leaving me defenceless in the flagrant ignominy of a happiness that I was hiding from them. Yes, they grounded me. They have my lesson timetable and are watching when I come and go. [...]

But something in me has died. My initial revolt has been replaced by something else, like a small hard kernel, an invulnerable tumour. I've finally realized that it's the absurdity of the human condition: just that, incomprehension, impossibility mixed with sadness, but without weariness or resignation.

For an adolescent of 15 years, Alix had a spectacular flair for language. Her spelling was faultless, and she was already thinking about style. As for this thwarted romance, I have been told that she went on to hold an unwavering grudge against her mother. The ban opened the door to her first anxieties and depression. If her increased use of alcohol, tobacco and drugs, described in the letters that followed, was anything to go by, this crisis had certainly had an influence on her. Though I am not convinced that this was the only cause of her melancholy.

I listen with caution to the *a posteriori* analyses, but I make note of them.

*

SHE WAS CALLED Alix Cléo Roubaud, née Blanchette. I am certain there is no dash between her first names. On official documents the 'e' has an acute accent; on her gravestone 'Cleo' is written without one.

Everyone called her Alix. That's how she signed her name too.

The Brother

I spent months looking for Alix's brother.
I made a list of all the Marc Blanchettes in Ottawa, and I called them, most probably at the worst possible times of the day for them. Since their father was a diplomat, I wrote to the embassy. I did a lot of research on the internet. Nothing.

One day, on Facebook, Viviane, Marc's daughter – Alix's niece – popped up on a page dedicated to Jacques Roubaud. She seemed to have found out about her aunt's success and wanted to get in touch with the poet. I wrote her an email and she gave me the address of her father, who for me was 'the brother'. I had never considered that he might be a father, a husband, that his life could have carried on beyond Alix. I had never pictured a Blanchette family after her. I wrote to him for the first time in June 2011. We met on 11 November 2012.

I had contacted the people mentioned in Alix's *Journal*. He was the final person I wanted to meet, and the most important. I wanted to conclude my research with him. I had already spoken enough to friends, to Jacques Roubaud, to people who said they had known her and for whom I was an excuse to talk about her. Besides, some had only met her once, and knew next to nothing about her. A number of the meetings had been of no use for my research. In my initial rush to get to know her, I was eager to have all the details – what clothes she wore, her habits, the books she read. But these accounts soon began to contradict one another: I would never have everything. Yet he, the brother, had lived with her, almost without giving it any thought. He would be able to tell me more about her and the constant moving of the Blanchette family. No opinions, just memories.

We arranged to meet in a café on rue Vieille-du-Temple in the 4th arrondissement in Paris, the street where Alix used to live and where she had kept a place of her own after moving to rue des Francs-Bourgeois with Jacques Roubaud. I immediately hoped I would be able to see the apartment. Friends of Alix had spoken to me about it: she held parties there on the first Wednesday of each month, it was the setting of Jean Eustache's film *Les Photos d'Alix*, and she had set up her darkroom there. This was where she wrote her journal and spent nights smoking and working before returning home to Jacques Roubaud – one street away – in the early hours.

Sans titre, portrait of Marc Blanchette taken around 1980.

I didn't know whether the family had kept the apartment, whether the location of our meet-up was down to chance or not.

THE ONLY PICTURE of the brother in the collection is a photograph taken by Alix: a slightly embarrassed young man standing in front of the camera, his upper lip covered in dark fluff. It is a relatively ordinary image, a family photograph. What kind of adult was he now? What would he look like? Marc Blanchette, born 1957, was certainly no longer that boy in the picture with mid-length hair.

He was sitting at the back of the café, next to his wife. I knew it was him from the way he was waiting, with his eyes on the door. I introduced myself and we immediately started talking about her. They were both staying at Alix's, and they had decided to carry out some work to freshen up the place. He clarified my timeline, which was practically non-existent for the period between 1952 and 1967. I knew almost nothing about Alix's early years. I learned that she had lived in Mexico until she turned four, then moved to Egypt for a year until 1956, and South Africa until 1957, before going back to Canada from 1959 to 1961. Then Portugal, Greece, and Ottawa again. After that came the personal recollections, the anecdotes that form the basis of the memories we have of people. For example, she called her brother *poisson-chou*,* and made fun of the utopian ideals of the 1960s – mainly love as a solution to conflict – which she deemed naïve.

ASKING OTHERS to give us fragments of their past is always risky and awkward. To summon up the memory of a beloved sister who has died, almost 30 years later, is to impose a certain violence on those left behind. There were lots of silent pauses, things that were impossible to say, the difficulty of allowing the

---

* *Translator's note*: This quirky nickname translates as *chou*-bun-fish, the '*chou*' often used in French as a term of endearment.

memories to surface and replaying them for the stranger that I was to them. His wife slipped into these pauses to explain their pain, the presence of this sister she believed she could see in her daughter's liking for photography, in the oval shape of her face. This *pas de deux* was a relief for the brother, allowed him not to have to say everything, not to repeat it all. After lowering his head for a few minutes, filled with emotion, his mind seemingly elsewhere, he continued. Her death – a pulmonary embolism – was still a mystery to him. He mentioned suicide, which had been a temptation since her teenage years. In 1982, when the Blanchette family was together at Christmas for the last time, Alix had seemed strange to him, radiant and distant, obsessed with angels, he said. But he put just as much emphasis on her sense of humour, her intelligence, and her mischievous bond with Jacques Roubaud. He broke away from the sad, morbid image of her that has grown from the *Journal*. There is more to see than melancholy.

He spoke to me quietly, with the gentleness of those who don't try to impose themselves on others, the calmness of witnesses who don't feel the need to analyze, to justify their words with vague theories. Alix was just his sister.

AFTER DINNER I asked to see her apartment, where they were staying while in Paris. I had already spent some time dawdling outside the large wooden door of 64 rue Vieille-du-Temple, stuck outside in the street without an entry code. As always when I get close to places where I sense a sudden geographical alignment with Alix, I had a feeling of apprehensiveness. I don't know whether I fear or hope for these meeting points where we share a presence in the world, briefly inhabiting the same perceptual space. I imagined that she would be there, on the other side of the door. Instead, I discovered a cobblestone courtyard adorned with plants, which we walked across. We went into the stairwell; her or rather their names were still on the letterbox, on the right, one typed, ROUBAUD, the other handwritten, stuck just below, BLANCHETTE. The apartment is on the third *and a half* floor. I was tickled by this detail, which I already knew of: a place between two floors, at a remove from the architectural norm. Without it the scale of the building would be unchanged. One of Alix's lovers, who had lived with her in this apartment, had drawn me a map, and described the kitchen and the dining room. I knew the layout of it without ever having been there; an impossible sense of familiarity surrounded the building.

Her handwriting appeared again on the door, with 'Blanchette Roubaud' written in black and red felt-tip pen. The brother let us into a small corridor. I immediately recognized it, for certain this time. I was able to point out all these things I had never seen before: postcards of Morris Louis paintings pinned onto the brown canvas covering the walls of the hall; in the living room, on the left, the chair from her self-portraits; the fireplace that served as the backdrop to Eustache's film; the wooden floor from the photograph *Correction de perspective dans ma chambre*. Nothing had changed in 30 years. The family hadn't been brave enough to sort through her things, to sell or give anything away. Her belongings were all still there: a hat, a jacket, crutches. The sense of time suspended was dizzying – everything was untouched, left just as it had been in 1983, I thought, and yet I hadn't even been born then. My research had furnished me with fictitious memories. I felt like I was rediscovering what I had never known.

But renovation work was about to begin, the apartment was on the cusp of a new era. Stuck in the past for so long, it had only furtively existed in the present. My visit that day was the last time all of this could be seen: her, her space, a before. That was the last time I would be able to say, 'I'm at Alix Cléo Roubaud's place.'

In the bedroom, the bookshelf was filled with her books. Her brother sat on the bed, and I asked to have a closer look.

He invited me to look around, said he hadn't touched anything since her death. Under the bed, I found some papers, photographs and contact sheets. I didn't know whether she had put them there or if the family had decided to move them out of view, to place them outside the frame of memory and make the place a bit more breathable. I pulled out messy bundles, papers stuffed untidily into folders. When I looked up, I saw that they were tired from the evening, from this break with forgetting. The brother looked drawn, no longer managing very well to hold back his sadness or his weariness, his wish for silence. I left without being able to see everything, without even glancing in at the kitchen-bathroom-toilet where Alix developed her photographs at night.

I MET THEM AGAIN the next day outside the Centre Georges-Pompidou, where Alix's photographs were displayed in the permanent collections. They had come with a cousin and one of their sons, awestruck at seeing their Alix become a recognized artist. This was different. Unlike the previous evening, her presence was less immediate, tempered by the museum, daylight and anonymity. I showed them her name on the programmes and the two sections of wall dedicated to her on the third floor. We stayed in the room for a long time, looking at the 13 photographs. The brother laughed, recognizing his sister's sense of humour, the pleasure she got from shaking things up. I went through the pictures in detail with them and corrected some of the dates the brother came up with. I had an uncanny grasp of the timeline of events, for example, holiday dates, the day Alix left for France. Dates that don't belong to us are often much clearer than those which shape us.

Afterwards I took them to my place to show them the documents that Jacques Roubaud had passed on to me. The brother read letters Alix wrote to their mother, and some sent by his parents. Again, we didn't dwell for too long. These reunions that are initially joyful tend to become painful. Something Marc's son said stuck with me: 'We have to help Daddy learn to let it go.' He was right – let it go – walk away.

That evening the brother, Marc, gave me the keys to the apartment, so that I could sort through and archive its contents. He told me to take the books if I wished, because the link I was trying to forge with the past was exterior to me. He no longer wanted to hold onto the memories, and I wanted to share Alix with the rest of the world.

I spent nine days and some of those nights in the apartment, putting the documents that were there in order. In this space, Alix's space, before the family began works to transform it, I drew a line under the past that had remained in order to untangle it once and for all from the present.

Darkroom

THE FRONT DOOR to Alix's apartment opened onto a two-metre-long hallway, which led to the living room on one side, and to what had been her darkroom on the other. This room on the right of the corridor, simultaneously a kitchen, WC and bathroom, defied architectural logic. The sink and the hob were opposite a shower cubicle. At the back of the room, the toilet was just about hidden behind a sliding partition. Though not the most practical living space, this would have been ideal for a photographer: without any windows and benefiting from both a sink and a washbasin, photographs could be developed here with ease. Some trays could be placed in the shower, and others on the ground. The dining room, with its large window, was separated by a door, leaving the hallway windowless and completely untouched by light.

This apartment was where Alix developed most of her images, often late into the night. After she married Jacques Roubaud, she carried on coming to this former home converted into a studio. In letters, she wrote that she worked for up to ten hours on a single print. Not content just to expose, develop, stop, fix and wash photographic images, she also made use of mattes, mixed inks in chemical baths, applied toners, and scratched her negative or drew on the photosensitive surface.

For Alix the darkroom was a crucial step in the material and symbolic making of a photograph. Everything that happened before that was of little importance. The quality of a photograph depended very little on the shot itself. It was at the developing and printing stage that Alix came close to the final work. Negatives were insignificant to Alix, materials over which she didn't claim any ownership – she even used other people's films. This 'painter's palette' was always discarded. The only elements of the work process present in the collection are a few contact sheets, around ten positives, and some proof prints that probably only survived because she died suddenly.

Alix didn't want any posthumous works; she alone was to develop her photographs. Even if some negatives were found and developed, the new prints produced would be imitations. This makes Alix's works precious; their rarity makes them more valuable.

OTHER THAN A SINGLE course at the photography school in Arles, Alix was self-taught. Her technique improved with time, but the photographs are not all perfect: some pictures are askew, some poorly washed, others overexposed. She produced several trial runs before reaching the final print; her practice was exploratory. There might be up to 20 variations from a single negative, and she only signed the definitive print. For a portfolio she sent to the Paris Biennale, Alix had the images for *Si quelque chose noir* printed by professionals. These prints are immediately recognizable. Their paper is shinier, not as thick, and their edges are perfectly straight; the negative isn't visible in any part of the image. Perhaps the quality of their craftsmanship is more consistent with the idea we might have of an exhibition print, but they are lacking Alix's touch. For all her other applications and her exhibition at Créteil, she made the prints herself. These are more finely worked: the range of blacks is more extensive, the light infinitely varied.

In her studio, Alix developed original tools and methods which set apart the pictures that have passed through her hands. One of her discoveries was the *pinceau lumineux*, a 'light-brush', which allowed her to draw on the light-sensitive paper, producing a layer of black grooves. The term *pinceau lumineux* calls to mind the etymology of photography – writing with light – and defines the photographer as someone who uses light as a tool. But it is also a term used in physics – 'pencil beam' – to denote a narrow beam of pinpoint rays. Technically, Alix used a torch:

> I use the term pinceau lumineux for that little device doctors use to look at the back of your throat, your ears, and other interesting body parts when they are lacking a diagnosis.

Sans titre (self-portrait with *pinceau lumineux*), circa 1979, Montfort-l'Amaury.

In a self-portrait made with a light-brush effect, shown at the start of Eustache's film, Alix is sitting on a bed naked from the waist down and holding onto an abstract black wavy line, drawn with her torch in the darkroom. There is a man standing in the open doorway. The right side of the photograph comes from a negative taken by someone else; the left side, which is entirely Alix's invention, was created during the development stage. A number of shots were taken at this overtly sexual soirée. Alix, another woman and a man are together, half dressed, in a room that is practically empty apart from a bed. The third person doesn't appear in the photograph reproduced here.

THE SCENE IS AN UNLIKELY ONE: a thick figure standing in the doorway is holding his belly or his penis. He appears frozen, so much so that in Eustache's film, *Les Photos d'Alix*, Boris asks if it is a painting. Alix is looking at the camera, her body in profile, her head at a three-quarter angle. She is only wearing a jumper, the back of which is covered in feathers. She pays no attention to the man behind her; the protagonists of the photograph seem to exist in distinct spaces, two separate moments artificially stitched together.

SOME OF ALIX'S ACQUAINTANCES told me that she took part in orgies before her marriage. This scene, as strange and risqué as it may seem, did indeed take place. I don't know anything about the circumstances or some of the people who were part of it. In the photograph, murky reality collides with the fiction invented with Alix's light-brush. She looks like she is waving a piece of fabric, a dark material that conceals the ends of her arms. But the cloth has been replaced by a smoky, charcoal shape. In the darkroom, Alix decided to depict herself brandishing a wave of light.

Before taking up photography, Alix, who was raised by a painter mother, tried her hand at drawing and watercolour painting. In her texts, she reflected on the links between painting and photography, to understand the defining features of her medium by comparing them to those of the other arts. The American Abstract Expressionist movement in particular was often cited in her work. She paid homage to two major figures from this school: Jackson

Pollock for action painting and Morris Louis for colour field painting. During trips to New York in 1976 and 1978, she saw works by these two artists. There were two postcards of acrylic paintings by Morris Lewis, shown at the Guggenheim Museum, pinned up in her apartment. In January 1982, she went to the Jackson Pollock retrospective at the Centre Georges-Pompidou. In his essay *Modernist Painting*, Clement Greenberg, the New York critic who contributed to the triumph of Abstract Expressionism, stated that painting must return to its intrinsic qualities: colour and two-dimensionality. In a similar vein, Alix focused on the founding principle of photography in the darkroom: chemistry.

The streaks produced by the *pinceau* enable her to consider her movements, to be conscious of her gestures. Alix sought to leave a trace of her living body in the image. In December 1980, she noted in her journal:

> Photography is similar to calligraphy in the repetition of an exercise that aims to achieve the pure instant;at least that's the case for straight photography and its aesthetic;That's how despite its realism which is in complete opposition to painting,it is nevertheless close to gestural painting.Jackson Pollock also tries to retain the pure instant of the moment of production.Personally,I try using the light-brush.

In the darkroom, she wanted to produce the instant, like Jackson Pollock. Alix is likely to have seen Hans Namuth's photographs and short films recording Pollock in his workshop in the full swing of his creative process. The artist appears to get lost in the canvas, caught up in a sort of turmoil, sketching out a brute choreography; he is one with his creation. Alix inhabited the photographic paper in the same manner, trying to turn a photograph into an action.

For the series *Alcools, hommage à Morris Louis*, Alix used different methods, mixing coloured inks with silver salts. Like the painter, she abandoned her brush to practise symmetry and drip techniques, allowing raw colour to settle directly on the surface.

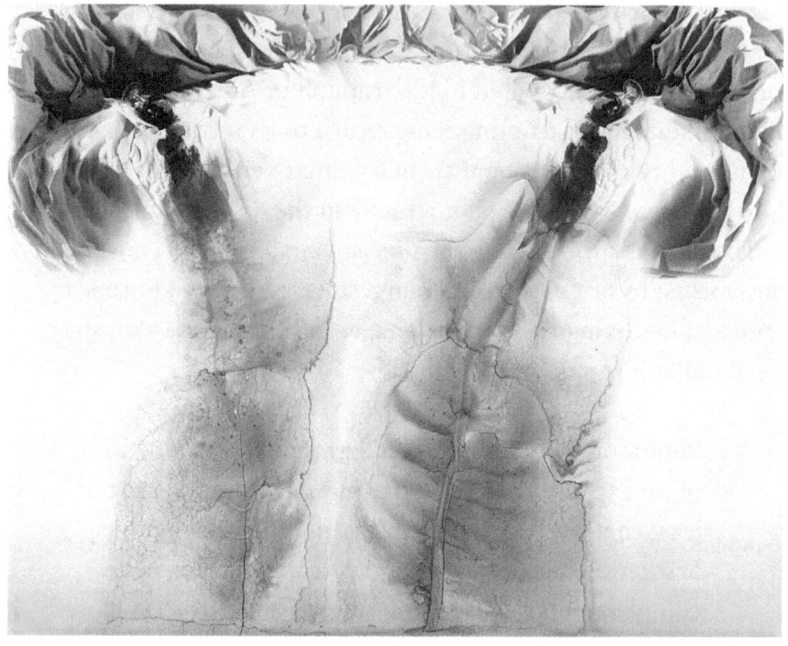

Sans titre, from series *Alools, hommage à Morris Louis*, December 1980.

A mysterious, macabre flow runs through the images. Also in December 1980, Alix mentioned her alcoholism several times in the *Journal*:

> Giving up drinking,such a hard thing.and taking sedatives,and sleeping pills.this is how it all started before:against the deafness and silence,the silence of tranquilisers,the infernal noise,tearful or hilarious,of alcohol,and often enough to go on;false

oppositions:drinking or smoking;suffocating or speaking;shaking in the morning or struggling to breathe;inviting sympathy for your asthma or being pitied for your alcoholism.

Alix gives a more literal dimension to the Tachisme technique (derived from the French word *tache* for stain) used by Morris Louis: in her photographs, a glass knocked over on a bed spills its liquid contents over the sheets. But unlike in the painter's canvases, the subject has not been expelled from the picture. The dizzying effect of these photographs simulates the intoxicating giddiness of the wine or whisky that Alix drank in considerable quantities.

The pictures in this series seem to be stirred by a rippling undercurrent. One of them shows a repetition of the same overturned glass, a mise en abyme; the photograph is no longer enclosed by

Sans titre, from series *Alcools, hommage à Morris Louis*, December 1980.

the frame, reproducing itself *ad infinitum*. The folds of the sheet create an echoing effect and give this photograph an almost sonorous quality; it still resonates with the moment of its creation.

    The darkroom was an ambivalent space. Alix could spend long hours there, enthused and focused. On days when she was feeling downcast, she feared shutting herself away. But she never gave up this place that was strictly hers, this place that held the destiny of her photographs. Photography is a nocturnal, solitary activity. While waiting for a print to develop, she would write a letter or her journal on her typewriter. Sometimes the telephone would ring: Jean Eustache often called her in the middle of the night. When I went to her apartment, I found what was left of this laboratory: stored in the cupboard of the large room were her tanks, her enlarger (an AHEL 67), an easel, a glazer and storage cases for negatives. The place's raison d'être was still present, but covered in dust, fallen into disuse.

Bookshelves

ALIX CLÉO ROUBAUD'S bookcase was still full when I went to her apartment. However, I found almost no trace of Gertrude Stein or Ludwig Wittgenstein, which had been key reading for her. I learnt that Alix's mother, Marcelle Blanchette, had decided to part with the books at the beginning of the 2000s. Friends and academics who were interested in her work bought some of the books, others were sold at Gibert Joseph and other second-hand bookshops in the 5th arrondissement in Paris. Even then, 524 books remained.

First of all, I had to separate Alix's volumes from those left by other people who had stayed in the apartment, tourists or friends of the family. I swiftly pulled out the guides to Paris, the 'Things to Do in the Île-de-France' books, and some novels. Anything that had been published after January 1983 had to go. I then grouped the works by category: philosophy, English literature, poetry and politics, among others. I found some volumes from the Little Maspero Series,* a first edition of Deleuze's *Anti-Oedipus*, a lot of poetry, particularly Dylan Thomas, books on logic, and some essays on the history of Quebec. But not a single book on photography. Jacques Roubaud said that she didn't own any. Photographs, sometimes looked at in museums, were above all else to be made.

---

* *Translator's note*: Petite Collection Maspero is a series of social, economic and political works by left-wing and Marxist thinkers, published by Éditions Maspero between 1967 and 1982.

I covered each spine with a label 'ACR-MB' (Alix Cléo Roubaud – Marc Blanchette) to confirm the origin of the volumes. I classified and recorded them, definitively preventing any potential additions. It was 2012 when I suspended these objects in time. However, books are living things whose pages we turn down, annotate and scribble on. Alix often slipped in a wrapper, a newspaper cutting or a shopping list. For example, in the 'Comments' section of the inventory that I put together, one note reads: 'Handwritten annotation: Ottawa, signed on 14 February 1968 "from Raymond", underlined and annotated passages.' I don't know who Raymond is. In another book, the packaging of a drug for treating asthma marks the beginning of a chapter.

What should be done with these traces? It would certainly be fanciful to want to record all of them and keep the yellowing cardboard boxes. I don't subscribe to the cult of trivial habits that reaches its pinnacle in exhibitions where a pack of cigarettes, a bottle or an item of clothing is displayed behind glass. What do these reconstructions offer? I no longer need to gather evidence, my investigation is complete: Alix is dead, and her work must be kept alive. When I discover these tokens, after the initial emotion of feeling her presence, I see that they're unsuitable additions, and this is the real reason for my unease. Is there space to consider the banal in the archive? Give up these little trifles and fence off the collection, draw up the boundaries indicating where interest lies, scrape away the insignificant remains – is that what must be done?

TO ARCHIVE is to take stock of suspended time, to build the narrative of a piece of the past. In this sense the archive may be compared to the photograph as it is generally perceived: 'the ground for belief in reality', Alix used to say. A photograph is a witness statement. The pictures we take are all bound to a *before*; they constitute an illusion of re-remembering, the desire to keep hold of a moment in time, to possess it intact like a handful of water scooped from a river. A photograph means that the event did indeed take place and, at the same time, that it is over; it is both evidence and memory, the *that-has-been* at the heart of Roland Barthes' *Camera Lucida*. The archive and the photograph are twin sisters, machines that reproduce the past. The shutter release seals the instant, the death of the work. This is the only way it can be. The shots we take become our mental images, clinging to memory and becoming keepsakes. Today Alix is this collection, this bookcase, these photographs. Is there another way to think of it? Can we stop insisting that the past – or our view of it – be enclosed by such strict limits, like cordons erected around a crime scene, before it is offered up for consideration in the present?

Sans titre (portrait of Arthur Edward Blanchette), circa 1980.

In Jean Eustache's film, Alix shows a photograph of her father, Arthur, taken in a car. He is driving and Alix is sitting in the back, like the children seat-belted in for trips on holiday. She can only see his back, the back of his head and his arms. His hands are on the steering wheel, partly erased by the brightness of the white light coming in from the road through the windscreen. Of all the exterior, only one overexposed tree can be seen in the right-hand corner of the image. His forehead, balding temples and eyes can be seen in the rear-view mirror; there are also the thick-framed glasses which surround his eyes, just like the dark frame of the mirror contains within it part of his face. The vehicle is an enclosed, defined world of its own, everything outside it has been abolished by light.

AS EUSTACHE'S camera films, Alix explains that this image was taken in 1980:

> I took this maybe a year and a half ago. I took it because I realized then that was how I'd seen my father for almost all my childhood. When we travelled, when he was driving the car, I would always see him from behind. I only saw his eyes in the rear-view mirror. I saw his huge hands on the steering wheel most clearly of all. I trusted him. It's a sentimental family photograph. It's a childhood memory. But it's a childhood memory that we don't have in the childhood photographs, that's why I remade this photo. Well, why I re-photographed a memory that I had.

In the picture, she is replaying the past, capturing the world through her eyes as a child. Her father, seen by Alix as a little girl, is the main structuring element of the photograph. The landscape is unimportant. In 1972, Alix left Ottawa, her parents and her brother to go and study in Aix-en-Provence. It was a definitive departure: Alix only saw her family again from time to time, when her parents travelled to Paris, or on one of her trips to Washington or Tunis. This separation wasn't easy. Her mother found it difficult to be apart from her, her first child, her daughter.

Worried about the fragile health of her eldest child – the asthma in particular – she feared seeing her fall seriously ill. Up until 1980, the year of the marriage to Jacques Roubaud, she sent Alix several letters asking for news on her breathing, her weight changes, who she was seeing. Her concern was a combination of care and anxiety that often exasperated Alix.

Both women created images, rivals in the same field: the mother was a painter, the daughter a photographer. 'As a creator of images, the photographer is in competition with the painter and describes himself as an artist; as a chemist, he considers himself to be modern,' wrote Alix in her journal. She herself tried her hand at watercolours and inks, and she painted some of her prints. Catalogues for exhibitions of Marcelle Blanchette's work were stored carefully among her collection of books.

Sans titre (double exposure showing Marcelle Blanchette's face superimposed on portrait of Arthur Edward Blanchette), circa 1980.

In another version of the picture of her father driving, a double exposure, Alix adds in her mother's face, which appears to float in the car, watching her, the child and the photographer. The composition is exactly the same, her father's silhouette on the left, the rear-view mirror, the trees on the roadside. But this ghostly face, bodyless and translucent, restores the surrounding scenery. The road is no longer erased by light, making this photograph seem much more realistic than the first.

ALIX IS A FORGER HERE: she plays with the status of the photograph, producing the past by artificial means, and interfering with the workings of memory. In the initial version, she plays a trick on memory: it is a picture from 1965 taken in 1980. In the second one, she cheats reality. If photographs are usually subject to the passing of time, it is because they are truthful: you have to reach out into the world with your lens to produce them. But mothers' melancholic faces never float around in cars. And it is when Alix no longer appears in the frame that she distorts reality and photography disrupts the flow of time, failing to recognize, to discern anything, twisting. Alix captured the subjectivity of her memory: her mother as an illusion of retinal persistence, a shadow watching her in every memory. She wrote in her *Journal*, 'There is no space reserved for memory as there was in the past. There is photography as artificial memory.' This was also a mnemonic work that she had undertaken.

HER MOTHER is the spectre in the photograph, but roles were reversed on Alix's death in January 1983. It was now Marcelle who would have to live with the shadow of her daughter. When they were told of her death by Jacques Roubaud, the Blanchette family arrived in Paris to attend the burial at Thiais Cemetery, on the outskirts of Paris. Her mother shut herself in Alix's apartment for several days painting unusual portraits. On one of these imposing canvases hanging next to the bookcase, there are three depictions of Alix. One of them is a child, laughing, with her head tilted to the side. The other is pictured from behind, as though she were leaving, and the third from the front, in the foreground, watching us. Now she is the ghost from the car, the unreachable space closed off to the rest of the world, the past.

*

THE FIRST TIME I went to Thiais to see Alix's grave, I couldn't find it. I hadn't realized this was the largest cemetery in Europe. A few weeks later, a caretaker gave me the precise coordinates to locate it on the vast grid.

    Section 30
      Row 15
        Grave 42

Ludwig Wittgenstein

THE PHILOSOPHY of Ludwig Wittgenstein that Alix was studying inspired some of her texts on photography, but she never completed her doctorate 'Wittgenstein: Style and Thought – Remarks on Philosophical Writing'. Her university research on the subject was extensive, including critical readings of the *Tractatus logico-philosophicus* and analyses of other works, but no written draft of her thesis has ever been found. Alix used her notes questioning the relationship between language and image in an introduction to Eustache's film *Les Photos d'Alix*.

IN JUNE 1980, Jacques Roubaud and Alix were married in Cambridge. They stayed in the city for a few days. On 10 June, she wished to see the tomb of the Austrian philosopher, who is buried in the Ascension Parish Burial Ground. She took a photograph of the gravestone on which Ludwig Wittgenstein's name and dates of birth and death are engraved. The block of granite is surrounded by dark weeds that have wrapped themselves around its edges. A light-coloured plant runs across the picture, through his name. The grave is strikingly understated and looks like it has just been placed on the ground. The natural stone is worn and the indifferent grass and weeds growing around it don't set it apart in any way. This extreme simplicity gives it an impact which is in complete opposition to the pomp and splendour of some of the mausoleums reserved for great men, heaped as they often are with ornaments. This is a lowly, humble grave, resting on the earth.

Tombe de Ludwig Wittgenstein, Cambridge, 1980.

In 1984, *Banana Split* magazine published 'Photography; Wittgenstein; and the Rotten Apples'. The title was chosen by Alix to bring together a selection of her writing dating back to November and December 1981. Some of the ideas can be found in the introduction to Eustache's film, which was reproduced at the end of Alix's published *Journal*. The two texts by Alix, which I have included here, reflect on this extract from Ludwig Wittgenstein's *Culture and Value*:

> I just took some apples out of a paper bag where they had been lying for a long time; I had to cut off & throw away half of many of them. Afterwards as I was copying out a sentence of mine the second half of which was bad, I at once saw it as a half-rotten apple. And that's how it always is with me. Everything that comes my way becomes for me a picture of what I am thinking about. (Is there something feminine about this outlook?)[3]

PHOTOGRAPHY; WITTGENSTEIN; AND THE ROTTEN APPLES
Alix Cléo Roubaud

Text 1

1. Not only do saying and showing not overlap. but saying thinking and showing do not overlap.
2. Photography is based on: see that this is true. but in fact: at the time I was thinking of something else entirely.
3. To say is to make a proposition: a proposition is the image of a fact (of a showing): fact is to showing like the image before your eyes; fortune in the eyes of the player; love in the eyes of love. unlucky: failure.
4. Saying is the nostalgia of showing, inexorably banished from the image. Because you do not say an image; and you do not think it (you think of something else entirely); you speak about it; you use it. not grammar but logic. Fact. This fact is shown by the absurd.
5. But if there is absurdity, not all saying about showing is absurd. The overlapping of saying/showing under the watchful eye of thought is a monstrous coupling, a morganatic marriage where we do not know which of the two is the poor cousin.
6. The image does not think, does not speak. It does not put up resistance. Trivial or transparent, beautiful or insignificant, the photo attests to what is said by history; its condition of truth. the expression it's snowing is true when it is snowing; a photograph of snow resembles a saying because it is true, because for it to exist, the simple certainty that it snowed was required, even if you were thinking of the sun.

Text 2

1. But there is a problem: when saying and showing do not match up; in severing them, we produce a displacement of fiction (non-existent facts) truth (existent facts): if I speak about photographs that exist (you see them) and facts that have existed (I say they did), what is shown as proof of that is the photos. But they are not the <u>right ones</u>. not the ones we are talking about. That is if we are talking about what was thought. Fiction can give an account of Wittgenstein's paradox.

2. So who's lying?

3. Lies are supported by the invisible: that which shows but says nothing (you no more say nothing by showing your image than you say something by signing your name); that which says nothing, and only shows the incongruity of a saying that does not match up with what is shown.

4. <u>Effect</u> produced by the violent collision of saying and showing. Thus, the music of a film generally alerts us to the emotion we should be feeling; in general, image and sound each enhance the other. But what happens if the authenticity of the image is not denied (by a saying) but displaced; if what I say does not complement what is shown, but rather denies it.

5. And they must be photographs; not paintings (where anything goes).

6. And finally the paradox would be perfect if I am seen saying something other than what you can see.

7. That would be a film on 'the rotten apples'.

Jean Eustache

JEAN: Am I disturbing you? Have I woken you up?
ALIX: No, not at all, I was reading; I'm glad you called.
JEAN: I'm feeling really, really awful. I want to die. I've had enough of suffering like this. I feel like there's nothing left for me in this world. Do you know what I mean?
ALIX: Yes, I know what you mean. You were right to call me. I didn't think you would remember me.[4]

JEAN EUSTACHE and Alix met on 29 June 1979. Eustache's penultimate film, *Les Photos d'Alix*, was shot in a single take on 5 July 1980, on 35mm colour film, and edited by him from the 15th to the 25th of that month. In the film, Alix talks about her photographs to the filmmaker's son, Boris Eustache, using the pictures to support her narrative. The screening of the answer print at the LTC Laboratoires took place on 26 August 1980. Alix was unable to attend, as she was working on her big series *Si quelque chose noir* in the workshop belonging to her brother-in-law, Pierre Getzler, in Saint-Félix.

Filming took place at her home on rue Vieille-du-Temple in Paris, exclusively in her living room. A table was set up in front of the fireplace, where some of the books from Alix's shelves, dictionaries in particular, were laid out. Eustache interwove shots of her and Boris with inserts of the photographs gathered in a folder that the young man was handling.

Les Photos d'Alix is a short film made without a significant budget: a camera, a boom microphone and lighting. The film's opening and closing credits are shown manually by Boris. The names and copyright information were written out on sheets of white card by Jean Eustache, and his son reveals them one by one, just as he does with the photographs: they are in the same folder and, once they have each been filmed, the teenager turns the top one over, revealing the next card beneath it. These cards are signed J E. The handwriting, which is always the same – a signature, strictly speaking – helped me identify the few letters from Eustache in the collection. They all end with the same initials, two joined-up capital letters.

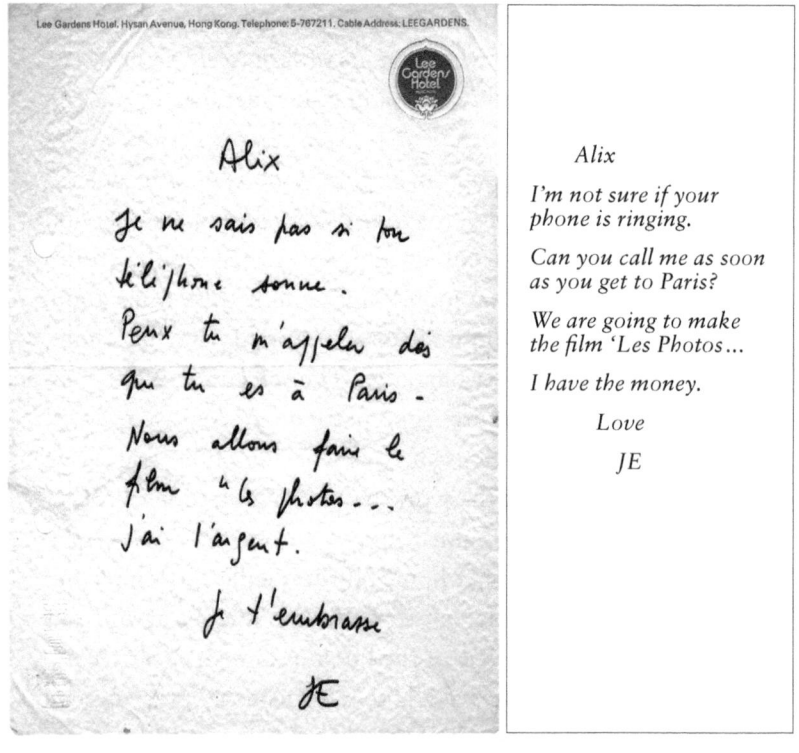

Alix

I'm not sure if your phone is ringing.

Can you call me as soon as you get to Paris?

We are going to make the film 'Les Photos…

I have the money.

Love

JE

Letter from Jean Eustache to Alix Cléo Roubaud, circa 1980.

AT THE START of the film, the two protagonists are standing in front of one of Alix's photographs that has been stuck on the dark canvas covering the walls. They then sit down on two chairs, which they don't leave for the duration of the film. Their conversation and the prints are the substance of the film: that is where the action is to be found. *Les Photos d'Alix* is as much about their discourse as the photographs: it is the combination of what is said with what is shown that gives the film its meaning.

Proceeding from the notion that images are silent, Alix and Eustache considered how to put them into words without explaining them, reducing them. They each in their own way endeavoured to explore ways of conceiving of the image and linking it to a discourse. In *Le Jardin des délices* (*The Garden of Earthly Delights*), filmed by Eustache that same year, Jean-Noël Picq describes and gives a commentary on the triptych by painter Hieronymus Bosch. He says what he sees, what it is about the painting that moves him. In this intimate ekphrasis, Eustache records a vision transposed into words, which emerges in fragments. Overall views of the painting are also rare, the director preferring individual detail shots of the many vignettes that make up the work.

IN *Les Photos d'Alix*, the images that we see on screen and, in the main, the words that reproduce them for us are hers. She names the people shown – 'a friend', 'my husband' – and the locations in the pictures – 'England', 'a pub', 'a hotel room'. But as the film goes on, what she says no longer coincides with what we see.

JEAN EUSTACHE edited the film over ten days. On 16 July 1980, Alix wrote in her journal: 'Had dinner with Jean who declares he is going mad editing the film;that he's never had such arduous work.' Indeed, what a job to disentangle the commentary from the images so that it no longer explained what the viewer was presented with, and without the viewer realizing. Eustache

Postcard written by Jean Eustache in 1979 to Alix Cléo Roubaud, with Pierre Bruegel's *Massacre of the Innocents* on the reverse (Kunsthistorisches Museum in Vienna).

'*A little sad / A little down / Melancholy / Kisses / JE*'

meticulously altered the soundtrack and the visuals. As the film goes on, Alix no longer talks about the photograph that Boris is showing us. For example, when a pair of shoes appears on screen, Alix refers to her first self-portrait. This leads the viewer to conclude that self-representation doesn't necessarily have to occur through direct figuration of the person. We come up with justifications for the growing inconsistencies, invoking metaphor and an original aesthetic approach, but when she talks about a glorious body as she looks at a photograph of a pillow, a sense of unease sets in. The situation becomes absurd. When the film is shown, the audience often laughs because the discrepancies between the sound and visuals are so bizarre. Perhaps the film is a condemnation of lazy art criticism that always seems to offer a standard response, regardless of what the image is. This effect thought up by Eustache shows how absurd explanatory discourse can be when it doesn't take into account the actual *seeing*. Should *Les Photos d'Alix* be understood as a commentary on the failure of art discourse? Maybe, but that's not all it is.

A portrait of Eustache and another of Boris – which appear to have been taken on the set – feature in the film, but Alix doesn't refer to them. Through this specular device the film in the process of being shot suddenly shows up in the photographs, like a mise en abyme, an underlying distancing effect. You have to watch the film for a long time for some sort of meaning to emerge.

TO EXPLAIN some of the photographs, Alix reveals the techniques she used, for example, working with second-generation negatives derived from prints, the *pinceau lumineux* and double exposure. She goes into the making of the photograph, what Boris calls the 'special effects'. But there is no forgery involved: it is precisely in this *doing*, the process, that photography exists. Traditionally, the shot, the *snapshot*, is aligned with reality. A photograph is necessarily true, because to make it someone has

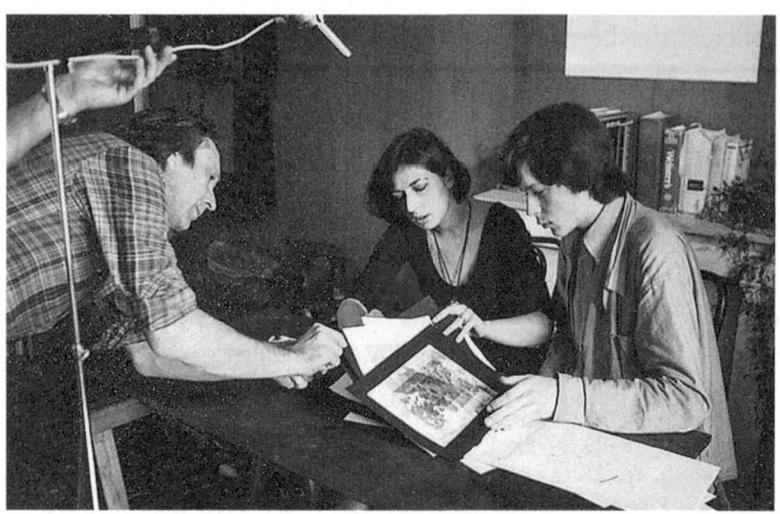

Jean Eustache, Alix Cléo Roubaud and Boris Eustache
on the film set of *Les Photos d'Alix*, 1980.

had to go into the world and extract a small piece of it. We don't take pictures of unicorns, although we might photograph a sculpture of a unicorn, and that has to be real – the image confirms its existence. You might capture a state of mind, an idea, but this will be done through something that tangibly exists. There is something concrete behind every photograph, and since each one bears witness to a real moment, it is inscribed in time. Photographs give us back a moment from the past and, for this reason, they are the ultimate avatar of memory. But that's not taking into account the craft of photography, chemistry and perspective, which have the power to distort perception. Alix was not seeking to produce snapshots, but pictures that were severed from reality and time. If Alix re-photographed a print, it was to make a photograph

> more photographic than the photograph, that is, more distanced from reality than it is, to make it felt that it is a photograph and not reality, and even less than reality and much further away than reality.

Eustache's film is a statement. Alix explains her theory of photography through her pictures. We have to look beyond the individual prints, and the sound-image discrepancy introduced during the editing of the film allows us to do that: it grants access to a level of thought that can be applied to all of her pictures, one which doesn't rely on anecdotal evidence. *Les Photos d'Alix* is a lesson in abstraction – a sort of inductive reasoning. Starting with individual photographs and their evident link with the artist's experience, we end up thinking about image in and of itself, the outlines of a concept. Alix doesn't speak about the prints that she has in front of her, but about photography. The synchronicity of the image, which appears to us in its entirety when we look at it, gives way to the diachronicity of the edited film. This progression of time, the real time of the viewer or that of the film, allows us to grasp an idea as it is developed, to follow a process.

AT THE HEART of this definition of the image is a lie. Alix and Jean Eustache introduce a playful device for us to think about:

> This film: saying and showing do not match up; in severing them we produce a displacement of fiction (non-existent facts)/truth (facts that exist): I'm talking about photographs that exist, and the facts existed; now what is shown as proof of that are photos, but not the right ones. Not the one I am talking about. Asking whether a film like this says or shows is not the same thing as asking if what I say is true (which is not in doubt and which the film shots of me and their documentary quality set out to prove); or whether the images, photos, are doctored; but it comes down to who is lying. And lies are supported by the invisible: the director who appears (but you don't say anything by showing your image any more than you say anything by signing your name) but

says nothing, and only shows the incongruity of a saying that doesn't correspond to what is being shown.⁵

Les Photos d'Alix is about the deviousness of the image, but most of all its tendency to be manipulated.

In December 1980, Alix wrote several texts on the film. Some were intended for a presentation for students at Paris-VII University, the others – notes, a typescript, research – were part of a wider project on the notion of the image. Two of these pieces of research are published at the end of the *Journal*. Alix drew up a list of numbered propositions in the style of Ludwig Wittgenstein:

1. Preliminary precautions.
2. Discourses on photography are naïve.
3. If the world is real, it is the sum of all traces.
4. The image is the ground for belief in reality.
5. Every photograph is a memory.
6. The only true photographs are childhood photographs.
7. All photographs are me.
8. Everything that can be shown can be done so clearly.
9. We photograph what is perishable.
10. Finally, photographs are sentimental.

These texts, inspired by the work carried out with Eustache, are evidence of her philosophical research on the image, but they are only one part of it. These statements, which at first glance seem obvious, are in reality complex and radical. Contrary to what was maintained by the 1980s wave of semiotics, Alix states that the image is not a language. She is also thinking about photography and its link with the other arts, particularly painting. In her opinion 'the reproduction of what is seen' and 'the proof and trace of an instant' are not sufficient definitions of photography. She gives as an example Johannes Vermeer, who created some of his canvases using a *camera obscura* – reproducing that which is seen – or, on the other hand, Jackson Pollock and action painting, which displays the substances that have been thrown onto the canvases, the present of the artist's craft – the proof and the trace of an instant. Alix lays the groundwork for a singular definition of an aesthetics of photography, which nonetheless remains incomplete.

In *Les Photos d'Alix*, she scatters these axioms throughout her dialogue with Boris. At the end of the first sequence, before the opening credits, she says to him: 'But in any case, the only true photographs are childhood photographs.' The statements are most resonant when delivered in her particular intonation, with a sense of humour hidden deep within them.

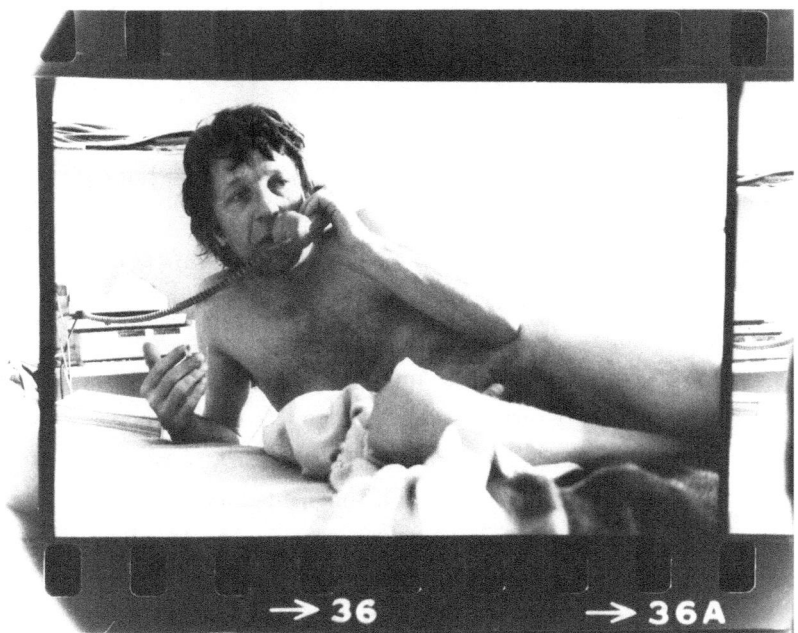

Sans titre (portrait of Jean Eustache), 1980.

VOICE, SPEECH (conversation on the nature of the image or discussion), was a recurring theme in Eustache and Alix's relationship, not only in the film, where it was held up and examined against the image, but also lived day-to-day during their frequent telephone conversations. Alix loved speaking on the telephone in her apartment-cum-darkroom and Eustache recorded their conversations. She took her phone off the hook when she wanted to be alone, and he sometimes called her when he wasn't doing so well. This was a simple rule she frequently mentioned and around which their relationship was structured. I learned of this routine from some documents that have been kept in the Alix Cléo Roubaud collection. One file in particular, which I found during the course of my research, shows the bond they shared, and includes transcriptions of some of their exchanges. It is essentially a script written by Alix for Eustache, which tells the story of when they met in 1979 and the beginning of their relationship. She brings up a telephone pact made during a call at three o'clock in the morning, after their first night spent together:

A: But when you're in a bad place, is there someone you can call? Someone you can always get hold of?
J: ...No. No, I don't think so.
A: Nobody? Really? Someone you can always count on? Someone you can always reach?
J: No.
A: Okay, well listen to me, and what I'm about to say is deadly serious: you can always call me when things are bad, and I don't want you to hesitate to do it. And I can see to it that you can always reach me whenever you need to.
J: But I don't want to bother you with that.
A: I know what it's like to be in a bad way at three in the morning and to want to kill yourself.

You know that, don't you? Call me anytime, day or night. Okay, I'm not saying I'm always doing great either, but I have a simple rule, I take my phone off the hook when I don't want to be disturbed. What do you say?[6]

THE DIALOGUES that make up this script were written in a hurry and do not have the same quality of writing as other documents produced by Alix. Between scenes of their transcribed conversations, she has inserted extracts from letters or her journal, pauses in which she takes a step back and carefully analyzes the facts. After this conversation, she repeated the same episode – delivered solely in her voice this time – in a letter sent to a friend.

I appear to be in an unlikely romantic situation: a contract with a suicidal man, the contract stipulating that he can call me day and night if he's having a bad time of things, but that I can take my phone off the hook if I'm feeling out of sorts.

Bypassing sexuality, bypassing romance even, I seem to be moving more and more directly towards death; the phantom death of another person, taken in hand in a way, which for the time being masks the shadow of my own death, which I was courting like you might court a woman. — I keep a calm but close watch on him (the suicidal man), without him being too aware of it; I'd rather he didn't feel any guilt on my behalf; I know how we kill ourselves when crushed with guilt. Anyway, and his therapist is going on holiday in August like everyone else: I might be busy.

Sans titre (portrait of Jean Eustache), 1980.

The conversations with Eustache were grim exchanges and often violent if we are to believe what Alix wrote ('little bitch, go fuck yourself'). The one I was able to listen to seemed mainly slow to me, heavy voices, thick silences – a broken exchange between two presences who had nothing to say to each other but were conscious of the emptiness within that separated them: a hollow proximity over the telephone. However, in letters to her family, Alix wrote enthusiastically about her 'director friend', their evenings together, and the raincoat that Jean-Pierre Léaud wore in *La maman et la putain* (*The Mother and the Whore*, 1973) which Eustache gave to her as a gift.

WITH EUSTACHE, Alix talked about the image in all its forms – the television that remained switched on without sound, the films he played for her – and about death. Their exchanges often revolved around suicide: he spoke to her about the turmoil he was in and Alix, as she frequently did, photographed Eustache as a corpse, offering him the image of his recumbent effigy.

Sans titre (portrait of Jean Eustache),
detail from a contact sheet, 1981.*

MOST OF THE PORTRAITS Alix took of Eustache were done while he slept. In this naked, unconscious state, he was fully submissive to her lens. Alix chose to leave a large amount of white space in these prints: the subject only takes up a tiny part of the photographic paper. Eustache therefore looks like he is surrounded by light, held in an all-encompassing whiteness. In one of these pictures, the director's sleeping body looks like it is surrounded by nothingness. The soft tones give this picture an unnerving calm, blurring the line between daily and eternal rest. Through photography she combines her wish to die with his. She inserted this passage into the script:

> (*A's Journal*)
>
> Photo of E. as a glorious corpse. The man who calmly feels he is going to die; very distant both from the world and from the white space of the paper that rises up like a shroud; a body withdrawn from the world, captured from behind; lovingly naked, sleeping and vulnerable, but also a corpse.

---

* This photograph was taken several months after *Les Photos d'Alix* was filmed. In the image, Jean Eustache is looking at a photograph from Alix's series *Si quelque chose noir*. His leg is in plaster following an accident in Greece in 1981. On 5 February 1981, Alix, who often mentioned Eustache's health in her letters, wrote to her mother: 'Jean Eustache needs a bone graft from his hip to his leg.'

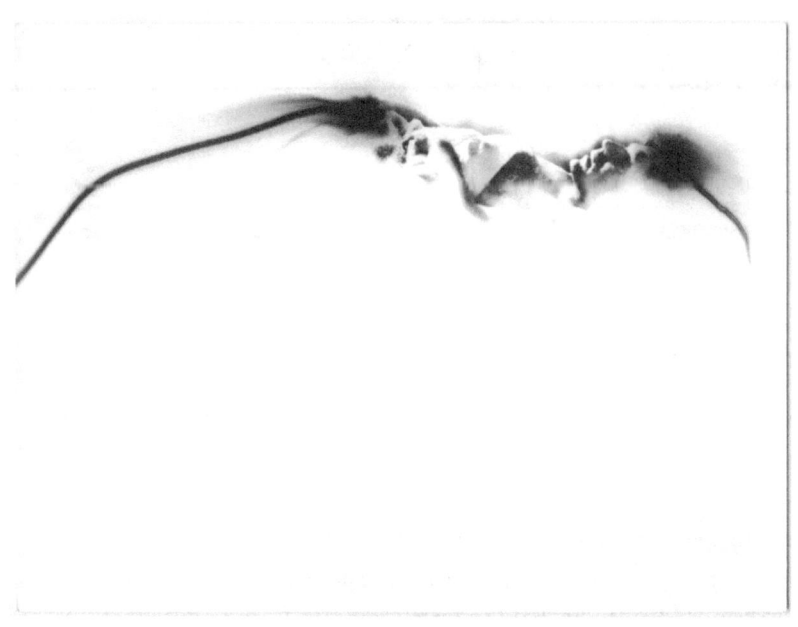

Sans titre (portrait of Jean Eustache), 1980.

Alix granted herself image rights in the style of ancient Rome, where they took impressions – death masks – of their illustrious dead and put them on display. The glorious body, she wrote of the picture of Eustache with his back turned, in the same terms she used to refer to the photograph of the pillows shown in *Les Photos d'Alix*:

> It's a suicidal photograph, a body that is, I suppose, mine, but glorious, dead. Finally dead but glorious.
> It's also quite a morbid photograph.

Death would therefore be a resurrection, for her as well as for him, a desirable state of rest for the body.

But Eustache's suicide on 5 November 1981, although foreseen, crushed Alix and her sinister predictions. Death is not like the pictures.

Jean's face in the morgue, his mouth slightly open, teeth that I didn't recognize. yet in the photos of him sleeping, his mouth was also open like that; what is it then that I didn't recognize, if not this very thing?

Alix was not present at his death, as some have claimed. She had spoken to him on the night he died, but before the fatal gunshot. After his death she continued to develop portraits of him, drawing trails that extended the body of the deceased with fictitious lines across the empty space of the page, transforming his human matter into black light. In her journal she wrote of the silent telephone that reminded her of Eustache.

I am your memory. The words that you utter to angels at night, without remembering them, and which I will make a note of. No greater loyalty. The pictures that you don't see. The words that you don't hear.

Your amnesia. I will be your complete archive; your photograph library; your tapes; your books.

And, one day, your fading into oblivion.

Bearing Witness

Alix's *Journal*, published by Éditions du Seuil in 1984, was the only record we had before the discovery of her letters, her essays on theory and her prints; it is also the best-known. Her words, her impressions, are recorded in it without reserve – it is both a truthful and literary document, a mix of fact and poetry. But like any book, it is a constructed text. And it wasn't Alix who put her writings in order. Like many private journals, this work was published posthumously by the person who was closest to her: Jacques Roubaud. It is therefore he, the husband-poet, who organized – shaped – her memory.

The *Journal* is the point of departure, the first encounter with Alix for those who didn't know her. It takes us to the very heart of her life and her writing, but it isn't everything. Jacques Roubaud selected only the final years of this personal account she had begun writing during her adolescence: 1979-1983, the years they spent together. From within this range, he excised the passages deemed too personal, some of the more sensitive content, and revelatory accounts that might have been hurtful or compromising for contemporaries of Alix. He limited his choice to the period in which he played a role in her life, most likely through a sense of propriety. Although the rest of the text has been placed under seal with a notary until such time as the names mentioned in these passages are no longer with us, Jacques Roubaud has chosen to offer the reader a few previously unpublished extracts in his afterword to this volume. We mustn't forget about the gaps, the omissions; not in order to protest about those parts of the text that are missing, to complain that we, as readers, have been denied them, but to remember that the picture provided by the *Journal* is incomplete. Personal accounts must be questioned, held at a distance, and eventually we must move beyond them.

Only three years of her notebooks have been published, and yet we call it 'Alix's journal'. So, nothing exists before 1979, the beginning of their relationship? Alix's life has become so closely associated with Jacques Roubaud's that previous events are not counted; everything is reduced to their story. In wanting her work to be seen, Jacques Roubaud became inextricably linked to it. So much so that Alix is often just the dead wife of a great writer, her marriage thus eclipsing her work. At best, she is the muse for whom he erected a tomb in his poetry collection *Quelque chose noir*. That is not what he wanted, sometimes he would have liked to be the husband of the great photographer, reduced to his conjugal role.

THIS IS NOT the only example of her work being pushed aside. Just as Alix was in Jacques Roubaud's shadow, her photographs were subordinated to the text: Alix's photographs have become tied to the *Journal* even though it was only intended as a way to bring them to a wider audience. Reproduced in the volume, they had no autonomous existence until the first exhibitions in 2009. They were nothing more than another aspect of the autobiography, a way of telling her story. Tied to the book in this way, they have often only been seen after or through it. We look through her pictures wanting to find death, suicide, loneliness, alcohol, and sometimes Jacques. It is a perfect match, the image and the text are one. But the collection is much vaster and shows that the pictures are not solely anchored in the personal. There are studies on repetition, inspired by

Gertrude Stein, others on reality and time, on the very ontology of the photographic image.

We must think of the *Journal* simply as an opening, and remember that it is through it that everything begins, if only our memory of her. The journal is the only thing, along with Jacques Roubaud, that has fought against her being lost forever. It is an object that must survive – her, him – a trace. With this document Alix cannot be erased. Jacques Roubaud had to be persistent, as Alix didn't have the time to make a name for herself. She died without knowing success; supported by her loved ones, but turned away by art dealers and critics, the steps she took to present her work in galleries never led to anything much. A year before her death, discouraged and disillusioned, she wrote:

> No press coverage for *Si quelque chose noir*.
> Rejection from the '82 Biennale.
> No desire to peddle the photos around galleries change profession,or find one even.

While Jacques Roubaud had published several books, some very well received by critics, Alix continually questioned the validity of her work. 'I wanted,wrongly,to be a writer.Marrying a poet was the way to not be one,' she wrote. Knowing her husband's talent, she despaired of her own. Faced with so many possibilities – a university career, translation, photography – she was unable to choose one. She had regular periods of crisis:

> I am a complete fraud not a photograph even books terrify me reading the silliest detective novels drives me into a panic drunk at night endless nights talking to Jacques no more passport a bank statement that says nothing to me overweight and ageing and the weight is only alcohol no thesis no phone calls why should they.

She lists a multitude of failures – the photographs, her body, her university work. Why did Alix give up on her thesis? The *Journal* gives no explanation of the reason. Those close to her mentioned her inability to understand German, illness, a feeling of failure and weariness. Be that as it may, Alix can't have given up without great sorrow.

'SHE WAS, essentially, a photographer,' the back cover of the *Journal* tells us, highlighting a choice she made towards the end of her life, that of the image. But what was the basis for this choice? Not necessarily a positive desire, but a series of abandonments and doubts. The writing in her journal remains key to my research. But it was through photography that she was able to be free, autonomous; it is a solitary practice. In some of her photographs, typed fragments cover the surface of the photographic paper. The image will never be completely free of language, even if only as the medium through which it is conceived.

Sans titre, from series *La Dernière chambre*, 1980.

IN THE PHOTOGRAPH *La Dernière chambre*, Alix layered one of her texts over the image. The last bedroom – the one in her parents' house in Ottawa, where the picture was taken, or the one where she died on 28 January 1983? In the centre of the picture there is a slightly rumpled bed, on the left a satchel, a pair of shoes and a box of Franken Berry cereal which acts as a stand for a lamp – erased from view by its own brightness – and an alarm clock. Her black shoes in the foreground are not lined up neatly. On the right, you can see a wire, probably the one linking the light to the power socket, and the bottom of a painting. This space is almost monastic, already emptied of her presence, with only traces remaining.

In the title, there is no possessive used to refer to this room, lending the photograph a symbolic more than a nostalgic meaning. We leave lots of places behind, our childhood bedrooms, our apartments, until we stay in the latest one which becomes the final one. The words covering the shot seem to be addressed to a lover. This sentence can be made out in the middle of the picture:

> I grant this word – so clearly my fragile and constantly threatened abode – the ambiguous status on which all my hopes are pinned.

Writing was a space of refuge as well as being invested with love and hope. Alix shut herself away in her journal when she was depressed and kept a record of her pain. But she decided to give up this 'fragile and constantly threatened abode'. Officially she would be a photographer who wrote.

SEEKING OUT the figures in the *Journal* and speaking to those who had known Alix felt like the only way I could move past it. I wanted to collect various statements so as not to invent or distort. More than just witnesses, they were players in what they related; I immediately accorded them a stance of rationality and truth. I didn't consider the fact that these accounts couldn't possibly be neutral. Not all of these individuals were of help to me. Some, like her friend Dian, and Jacques Roubaud, enabled me to learn more about her. Other more interpretative accounts offered nothing more than opinions: Alix was a rubbish photographer, an idiot, a genius, for example. Some took my research as an opportunity to talk again about their memories of her, and their sadness, which surfaced in the middle of anecdotes they recounted. I won't name those people.

I had noticed one man in letters and dozens of photographs. He was very handsome – he had a youthful face, with a straight nose and plump lips. I realized it was W. thanks to a very faded caption written on the back of a portrait. Alix photographed him right up until 1979, but he hardly appears at all in the *Journal*. Yet they wrote to each other, loved one another, and lived together. It was Alix who left him – we have the rough drafts of her break-up letters. He cheated on her, prevented her from working, from living, she wrote. On her return from a thermal spa in La Bourboule, she found him in their bed with someone else. Alix was more shocked by his poor manners than his betrayal.

I wanted to see him, to speak to him. He was certainly one of the men who had meant a lot to Alix, along with Jean Eustache and Jacques Roubaud. I called him and a woman answered. I explained my research. He immediately asked for the handset and spoke to me for almost an hour. I didn't understand any of what he was saying. He came across as confused, cultured, emotional, but above all drunk.

I met him a few days later at his house in the 13th arrondissement of Paris. I remember going inside, intimidated, crossing a hallway to get to a living room full of books and papers. He was sitting slumped on the sofa, unwell, I thought. He was thin and didn't manage to stand but greeted me enthusiastically.

The interview went on for four gruelling hours, all recorded on a Dictaphone. I have only reproduced my transcription of the end of it here, the only time he really spoke to me about her.

> — I called her my little darling. The day she died Roubaud called me about the funeral. Have you been to see the grave in Thiais?
> — Yes. Alix took lots of portraits of you...
> — Yes, I have the photos here if you want. It's me who inspired her love of photography. I have a claim to something! My old Nikon camera got a lot of use. We even set stuff up in the apartment to develop prints at night, with a proper lamp... And the trips, do you know about the trips?
> — No.
> — We went to her family in Washington, and to my parents, I don't remember when. We were in Jever, which has the best beer in the world, her favourite. If you like, I'll call my mother to ask when exactly we were there. She writes everything in her journal.

He actually got up to phone his mother and ask when they stayed in Jever, a detail that wasn't of much use to me. At the start of our conversation, he had said to me, 'I'm still intact.' What was he trying to prove to me? That he'd been spared by time or by pain? As far as I could see he wasn't *still intact*. From my research I've learned that time spares nothing, it takes away, diluting memory. He was not the attractive man from the pictures and letters. I hadn't even recognized him when I'd walked in. The problem wasn't so much one of health, but how impossible it was for him to summon up memories and talk objectively about Alix.

— We have the date! 29 July 1987! he shouted,
    hanging up the phone.
— But she'd been dead for four years then.

I left. So, his mother also kept a journal. What are we to make of these forms of writing that we like to hold up as evidence? The facts had eluded me once again. As the spoken word was an elaboration on the writing – already an *a posteriori* construction – it upset the accuracy of what I wanted to establish, and it didn't satisfy my need for stories. We must accept, it seems, that nothing is intact.

They said

intelligent asthmatic abrupt strange
distant deceased funny tall cold insomniac
Wittgensteinian night owl independent overrated original
bilingual lost socialite suicidal serene a personality
haughty proud an acquaintance educated protective alcoholic amateur
incredible unique obsessive artist dedicated sick restless
cultured a victim beautiful gifted unpredictable reader aggressive
Canadian letter writer visionary
ironic photographer friend endearing brilliant
eldest child tormented Parisian way ahead bisexual exiled fantastic
fragile depraved married happy brunette lover dark slim
depressive dogmatic fascinating gone loved muse intellectual
ruthlessly ambitious forgotten unstable mistress
gifted egocentric on drugs broke old-fashioned stubborn secretive sensual playful
there for you a genius passionate solitary music lover
philosopher impressive desperate dead tragic attractive
poet a character talented

Doubling, Shifting, Repeating

> *You need not expect time to be solid.*
> *You might but you do not have to.*
> *And as you do not have to you do not.*
>
> Gertrude Stein [7]

THE DENSE THEORETICAL background to Alix's photographs was based on two systems of thought: the first, philosophical and logical, was Wittgensteinian, and the second was inspired by Gertrude Stein. Alix was influenced by the theory of prose that was Gertrude Stein's life's work. She read and studied the author from 1976, quoting her writing in epigraphs to several university essays. In 1978, she devised a documentary project on the life of Gertrude Stein. Her partnership with Jacques Roubaud, who was also passionate about Stein's work, nurtured this interest and helped it develop. In 1980, Alix accompanied him to the Gertrude Stein symposium that he organized with Gérard-Georges Lemaire at Cérisy-la-Salle in Normandy. In 1979, she worked on a translation of some of Stein's texts and produced a French version of the erotic poem *Lifting Belly* with Jacques Roubaud.

MOST OF ALIX'S work on Gertrude Stein was photographic. In 1980, she created the photograph *Deux sœurs qui ne sont pas sœurs*. The title comes from a screenplay by Gertrude Stein, the only French text in the volume *Operas and Plays*. The note 'film'

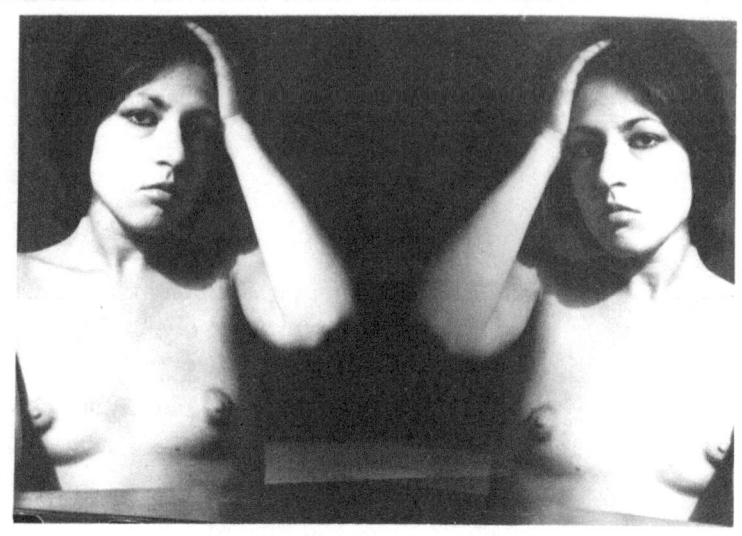

Deux sœurs qui ne sont pas sœurs,
circa 1980.

appears above the title. This screenplay, published in 1930, was conceived by Gertrude Stein as a sequence – it functions like a loop, a cumulative series of events. At the heart of the composition is the number two: the story features two laundresses, two poodles in a photograph, and two women in a two-seater car. The scene is repeated twice, with slight modifications.

Alix's photograph bearing the same title is a mirrored self-portrait: two Alixs appear, each positioned on either side of a central, vertical line of symmetry. The same dark triangle cuts through her breasts on the far right and the far left of the image. Alix uses the same principle structuring the screenplay – repetition, doubling – but does away with the narrative. This image is not an illustration of a text by Gertrude Stein, but a translation of the principles of her prose into photography.

LIKE THE EVOLVING screenplay, photographs are not exact duplications of their negatives. The figure on the right doesn't come into contact with the upper edge of the print, and more of her shoulder disappears into the space outside the camera's range. Her skin is illuminated by a more intense light, while her right elbow disappears into the darkness. It isn't the subject itself that changes, but the making of the image that transforms it. Chemistry and perspective distort this pair, the two Alixs are not consistent. Just as Gertrude Stein focused on language and grammar rather than narrative, so Alix worked on the possibilities of the photographic medium, on the properties particular to the craft. She mined a Steinian axiom – repetition – to create an image and add another layer to her ritual practice of the self-portrait.

The serial dimension to Gertrude Stein's work, the arithmetical reiterations, enabled her to find a continuous present in prose. Defined by a capital letter and a full stop, the Steinian sentence is a dynamic principle that keeps moving forward, like a continuous but sometimes irregular pulse. The phonetic shifts occurring through a single element of the writing give it movement, make it sing. Alix took the texts' rhythm and translated it into her photographs. In some compositions her body, like a word, comes back slightly changed.

ALIX WORKED on repetitive series and multiple self-portraits which produced variations. She made compositions from pictures of herself lying on the floor of her apartment, in which the same shots are repeated. A strange rhythm, both measured and frenzied, runs through these photographs. In the reproduction below, a single negative – Alix naked, looking back at the lens – is used five times; another where her face is looking upwards, four times. The density of the black shades and the opacity vary in each of the figures of Alix present. Her silhouette is at once similar and always renewed, altered little by little as it cascades through the picture.

Sans titre, from series *Correction de perspective dans ma chambre*, circa 1980-1981.

The series foregrounds repetition. Each picture reveals a jerky sequence of doubled figures of Alix and, together, the photographs form a whole populated by the same likeness. Contained within the sheet of paper on which it is printed, each piece is like the sentence marked out by its punctuation. Together they compose a Steinian landscape whose constant mutation produces a photographic real time.

ALTHOUGH AESTHETIC, the repetition is first and foremost the result of a theoretical approach. Alix observed the inevitable split of the photograph from the present, the slipping away of the image into the past once it has been developed. Gertrude Stein's attempt to create a continuous present in prose enabled Alix to find solutions. For the author every sentence is an instant; like photography, Gertrude Stein's prose is made up of time. And if

Sans titre, from series *Correction de perspective dans ma chambre*, circa 1980-1981.

a photograph is an action, it is because it is intended to exist in the present: a photograph encompasses a process, it is *photographing*.

Gertrude Stein wrote texts that were meant to be spoken and heard; reading her writing aloud is a sonic experience. Alix sought this musicality in the image: 'the singular to be repeated until it becomes a dance, until it sings'.[8] Gertrude Stein's ever-shifting sounds become Alix's dynamic photographs; in both cases a sense of morphological harmony produces repetition.

ALIX HAD a theoretical approach to photography, she conceived of her medium in a very particular way. But photographs don't tell us anything. We can only describe and reflect on what we see. Alix's photographs don't hold any meaning in and of themselves. I can say what I see, never what the pictures mean.

Lifting Belly

On Alix's bookshelves there was a copy of Michel Serres's work on translation[9] and the conference proceedings from a *Symposium on Poetry Translation*,[10] both carefully annotated. Alix, who was bilingual in English and French, was caught between these two languages, at times writing her journal in one language and sometimes the other; translation was a way of bringing them together.

She worked on Elizabeth Bishop's *Geography III* with Claude Mouchard and Linda Orr. The collection came out with Éditions Circé eight years after she died.[11] In 1980 she published a translated extract of Gertrude Stein's erotic poem *Lifting Belly* with Jacques Roubaud in the literary magazine *Action Poétique* no. 82/83. Alix and Jacques, both confirmed anglophiles, worked collaboratively on their translations, combining their poetic insight and linguistic virtuosity. On 19 December 1980, Alix wrote to her mother:

> Being the wife of a well-known writer who never answers letters nor the telephone would be a secretary's life if he didn't also encourage me and help me with my health problems, if he didn't do the shopping for dinner [...]; if we didn't complement one another perfectly in our sessions translating American poetry, he with his poetic diction, which is immeasurably superior to mine, and I with my English, considerably more accurate than his.

Alix's interest in Gertrude Stein, expressed in letters to her family from 1978 onwards, matched Jacques Roubaud's passion for Steinian prose. Here is an extract from their translation of *Lifting Belly*:[12]

Kiss my lips.	*Embrasse-moi. La bouche.*
She did.	*Comme ça.*
Kiss my lips again	*Embrasse-moi la bouche*
she did.	*encore comme ça.*
Kiss my lips over and over and over again she did.	*Embrasse-moi la bouche encore encore encore comme ça.*
I have feathers.	*J'ai des plumes.*
Gentle fishes.	*Gentils poissons.*
Do you think about apricots.	*Penses-tu des abricots. Nous*
We find them very beautiful.	*les trouvons très beaux. Il*
It is not alone their color it is	*n'y a pas que leur couleur*
their seeds that charm us.	*il y a leurs graines qui nous*
We find it a change.	*enchantent. Ça nous change.*
Lifting belly is so strange.	*Monte le ventre est si étrange.*
I came to speak about it.	*Je suis venu en parler.*
Selected raisins well their	*Raisins choisis bien leurs*
grapes grapes are good.	*grappes grappes sont bons.*
Change your name.	*Change de nom.*
Question and garden.	*Question et jardin.*
It's raining. Don't speak about it.	*Il pleut. N'en parle pas.*
My baby is a dumpling. I want	*Mon bébé est un beignet. J'ai*
to tell her something.	*quelque chose à lui dire.*
Wax candles. We have bought	*Bougies de cire. Nous avons*
a great many wax candles.	*acheté beaucoup de bougies*
Some are decorated. They	*de cire. Il y en a de décorées.*
have not been lighted.	*Elles n'ont pas été allumées.*
I do not mention roses.	*Je ne parle pas de roses.*
Exactly.	*Exactement.*
Actually.	*En fait.*
Question and butter.	*Question et beurre.*
I find the butter very good.	*Je trouve le beurre très bon.*
[...]	[...]

Embodiments

ALIX IS OFTEN NAKED in her self-portraits. Her body infuses the photographs with a sensuality that is sometimes careless, and at other times deftly managed. Her breasts, buttocks and vulva are shown clearly. From behind the lens, she undressed her lovers: Jacques Roubaud, Eustache, women I don't know. Sometimes she would play a role in the scene, performing the beginnings of a sexual act, with her hand around an erect penis, grasping, teasing and tormenting the flesh of other bodies. The sensuality of her work is simple and intentional: Alix's was a living body, her pubic hair thick and luxuriant; her encounters were entered into wilfully rather than endured. Alix was not a muse, but a voracious photographer.

The eroticism in her work is twofold: literary – as can be seen in the translation of Gertrude Stein's *Lifting Belly* and some passages from her journal – and photographic. Alix revealed her body in self-portraits, appearing serious or provocative, sometimes reflected in multiple mirrors. Some pictures depict an embrace, a tender moment of rest, and in others she sidesteps the event entirely, playing around with the space outside the camera's range, where visibility recedes.

Nudity is a constant feature of Alix's photography: she appears with her clothes off and allows her body to be seen. Photographed as well as photographer, Alix liked being naked. In *Quinze minutes la nuit au rythme de la respiration* (see page 111), her camera

Sans titre (Alix Cléo and Jacques Roubaud), circa 1980.

was placed on her bare chest. She was not the subject of the picture but removed her clothes to be in direct contact with her camera and the surrounding landscape. Her body is implicated in the making of the image.

ALIX WAS ANXIOUS about her figure – in her journal she recorded fluctuations in her weight, her skin condition – and this focus also shows a clear and conscious link with physical intimacy. Although she was ill, Alix inhabited her body in a way that was admirable. She asserted the fundamental freedom to make her own choices, to be a woman with desire. She made use of her sexual boldness, depicting herself suggestively beside men who were fully dressed, photographing herself in provocative poses. Appetite and pleasure were integral to her self-esteem, which was often hindered by illness and self-destruction.

Sans titre (Alix Cléo and Jacques Roubaud), circa 1980.

Nudity is all the more striking in photography when it is real, when it involves a person whom you know, or knew when they were alive. Alix played on this effect in some of her suggestive pictures, and on the realism of photography. Rather than a nude, she presented her nudity, without artifice or affectation.

The hotels she stayed in regularly were the ideal setting for these images. The fantasy dimension of the hotel room, an enclosed, anonymous and temporary space, revolving around a bed, conjures up a simmering eroticism. One picture, taken in Cambridge in May 1980, shows her alone, lying on a bed with crumpled sheets.

Le 31.v.80, University Arms Hotel, Cambridge (ch. 217).

Her legs spread wide expose her sex. Her left hand rests on her hip, while her other arm is folded back under her head. Her eyes are fixed on the lens, and thus also on the person who is looking at the print. There is a lustful, defiant expression on her face, which is raised by a pillow. Only the bed appears clearly, the rest of the room fading from view. The predominant grey is broken up by three black points: her vulva, her hair and the door handle, which has a 'Please, do not disturb' sign hanging from it. This triangle directs the eye around the image and tells the story of a woman who is indulging in solitary pleasure, her hand gravitating towards a caress. She is not to be disturbed and yet the viewer is plunged into this secret, sexual moment, taking her unawares, slipping into the room to become the voyeur who – at the risk of disturbing her – oversteps the warning on the door and looks at the central, unavoidable point of the photograph, Alix's sex, which she exposes like an enticement.

In her journal Alix said she made love a lot. In letters she laid bare her desire for her lovers. Before her marriage she enjoyed an unrestrained sex life with both men and women. At that time Alix often photographed her lovemaking, capturing the ambience of seduction or pleasure in these moments. She produced several portraits of the men and women she loved.

In the Alix Cléo Roubaud collection, an erotic contact sheet shows Alix and one of her mistresses. The contact sheet seems to me to be the perfect medium for sensuality, from both a semantic and aesthetic point of view. Technically, it represents the first stage in the darkroom process. After finishing a film, the photographer can print the entire roll out on one sheet. He or she then ends up with thumbnail images of every shot lined up in horizontal strips. This overview allows the photographer to choose the images he or she wishes to further develop and print in large format.

To make a contact sheet, you have to press the film against the light-sensitive surface of the paper and expose it; the technique involves direct contact, a photographic method described in playfully apt terms.

The finished contact sheet, which lays out a sequence, is similar to cinematic film. If the pictures on the roll are taken at the same time, a sense of movement runs through them, a momentum. And if the viewer imagines these images brought to life by the motion connecting them, he or she can watch a scene unfold. The woman in the vignettes is sprawled out on a bed, sitting or lying down, with her legs pulled in against her stomach, outstretched, or slightly open. She is only wearing a T-shirt and pale knickers. The rumpled sheets suggest that these images were taken after lovemaking. Appearing abandoned in some shots, in others the woman looks directly at the lens; she seems to oscillate between an ecstasy that thwarts the outsider's view and a flirtatiousness that plays up to the woman watching her.

Sans titre, contact sheet, 1979.

The images are blurred; it is almost impossible to make out her face. Some are completely unreadable: incomprehensible close-ups, shots taken sideways and upside down, not enough or too much light. It would seem that Alix didn't take the time to focus, to adjust her shutter speed, to compose the image. This haste betrayed by the technique implies that the photographer was troubled, restless. This contact sheet is a picture of desire, on both sides of the camera.

PHOTOGRAPHY ALLOWS YOU to catch a moment, to produce an object from unspeakable pleasure, and keep it. In her text for Eustache's film, Alix wrote:

> You can paint for love of a woman, write about a woman, sing about a woman. You photograph the one you love differently from how you write a poem about her or paint her; love exists in all these cases; but you photograph her to hold onto a moment of her, even an obscene moment, and the photograph is a sentimental object of the lover's, just like a lock of hair, a piece of clothing forgotten at yours; in short, it is a piece of her, and so, a collectable item. You have taken something from her, and this thing is not enough; you either have one photo of her or a thousand; she might leave you, but you can always keep at least that. The photographer is an obsessive collector. Photography is theft.[13]

For Alix, love photography is a means of extracting a moment in time, rescuing it from the flow of existence to keep hold of it. In this way, the photographic act is a form of possession. The semantic field of photography that includes 'aiming', 'taking', 'loading' and 'shooting' has been widely exploited by artists and critics. Michael Powell's film *Peeping Tom* centres on a young man obsessed with images, who pursues women to capture their death on film. He later replays these films of sexual terror at home, for his own pleasure. Photographer Miroslav Tichý's work was characterized by its voyeurism: he took hundreds of shots of women with a hidden camera. There are many such examples.

Alix made no secret of her desire to possess: the models posed, and she adroitly managed the subject matter of the photograph. The image is by its nature erotic, a fact she knew and wrote about:

> 25 Oct., 2.35 (am), coming back from dinner followed by a drink in the 5th, on foot in the rain, a little drunk, very high, slightly wet, perfectly alone

By what irony was I given a photograph of you this evening, which now lies on my floor in a yellow carrier bag next to the umbrella. I don't want to see it.

Immediate: you left for fifteen days.   Why   .
I miss your tongue, the taste of you, your   .

Why write to you, anyway? Wrote my most 'beautiful' letters to people that I didn't love. Which calls into question the notion of 'beauty': they were more written, better written, and what's more I've never known how to say that I love

Baby-faced pride? It took me a long time to see it, the pride, which takes on the dimensions of dignity, certainly unexpected in a baby face: a man who likes to plan ahead, you live in the essence of the future, which you expect to measure up to your expectations, and which you have arranged and determined beforehand. Unusual, in any case. Future made to order, love made to order   ?

My books; my friends; my mornings; my evenings; my illnesses; my apartment; my medicine

cabinet, my moods, my sexuality, my fridge: a whole little world that you know. In which you have a strategic advantage over me: all you gave of yourself was your own effigy thought: beautiful to the core.
In English the word *beautiful* as a singular attributive adjective is used in the same way as in French when you say: *quelqu'un de 'bien'*, a 'good' person. But good to the core?

Extreme irritation at desiring you in detail and knowing you almost in abstraction. But let's do it:

In this photo (which I've just taken out of its synthetic case) you are looking at the Courtauld Institute catalogue and frowning. A cigarette in one of your big hands, almost as big as your face, which is in fact compressed in the foreshortening effects of the light. Tender neck, throat, cut for me, fortunately, by the raised page of the catalogue. Bad luck, your other arm boasts a magnificent vein.

I dreamt about a photograph I had made and which I was looking for in a magazine at a newsstand: a photo of a man leant over a pterodactyl (perfectly) leant over a rotting carcass, in profile and against the light on a beach, and doubled by laying two negatives on top of one another.   Wanted, this morning, to tell you my dream. To say: hold your breath and suddenly
      (as strong as a hand slipped into a gap in your shirt in the photo)
      suddenly I'm telling you we are telling each other and you are held by the eye watching you, my eye

In this letter, Alix dreams up a picture, spots the features of her lover in the shot, and loses herself in it. The picture is the point of departure for her reverie, and the photograph she describes – nowhere to be found in the collection – was taken by her. The sexual dimension is therefore played out twice: when taking the shot and, later, looking at the picture.

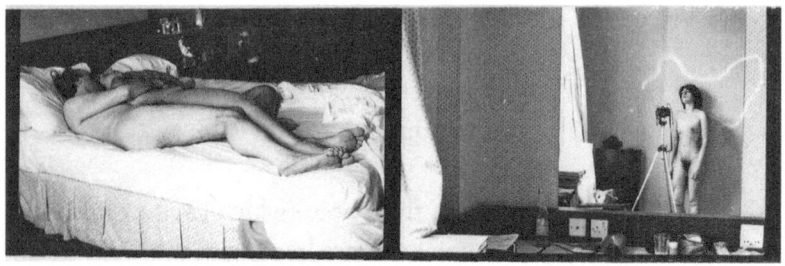

Sans titre (Jacques and Alix Cléo Roubaud on the left, Alix Cléo Roubaud on the right), detail from a contact sheet, 1980.

Most of Alix's erotic photographs were made with Jacques Roubaud from 1979 onwards. Their regular travel (Tunis, Cambridge, London) and the poet's trips to conferences and readings meant the couple would stay in hotel rooms in different cities. Alix often had her husband pose, reversing the concept of muse that artistic tradition is so attached to. In this case it was not the poet who would sing of the beloved woman, metamorphosing her in the heart of his compositions, but the photographer who manipulated the loved man and choreographed his appearance. Sometimes she would set the self-timer on her camera and slip into the frame.

There are several of these photographs of the couple, and Alix noted the place and the hotel room number on the back of each one. They form a number of short series – calm and gentle or overtly sexual – which clearly depict a happy marriage.

Sans titre (Alix Cléo and Jacques Roubaud), 1980.

VIII.80 *Saint-Félix* (Alix Cléo and Jacques Roubaud), 1980.

Le 14.v.80, Hôtel de France, ch. 15, Avignon
(Alix Cléo and Jacques Roubaud), 1980.

Sans titre (shots of handwritten texts by Jacques
Roubaud), detail from a contact sheet, 1979.

ALIX DIDN'T JUST PHOTOGRAPH her husband, but also some of the notes or letters he had written to her. On another contact sheet were photographs of three texts by Jacques Roubaud. They are love poems which were composed at the start of their relationship. The first, dated November 1979, is tender but distant: Alix and Jacques Roubaud had only just met. The other two, written in the first fortnight of December 1979, are erotic. A comparison of the dates shows that theirs was a whirlwind romance.

There are no prints of these photographs of texts. Perhaps Alix didn't want to develop them or didn't have the time to do so. Taking photographs of texts allowed Alix not only to keep a record of them, but also to make them hers, in a way. She actively took possession of them, by making images of them.

ALIX KEPT ALL the letters she wrote (she kept carbon copies) and those that were sent to her. In some of her prints, she layered texts she had photographed onto the images. This process was used in two different ways. She took passages from her private journal and combined them with her self-portraits, thus creating an image of herself that was between writing and photography; or she projected missives from her lovers onto the surface of the picture. Image and text thus formed two poles of a single print, two ways of possessing the beloved.

SUGGESTION IS EROTIC. Sketching outlines to be filled in and dropping hints allows the involvement of the viewer's imagination. In photography the space beyond the camera's range invites the arousal of curiosity. That which is outside the frame eludes the person who is looking. But the area just beside the image constitutes a diegetic space where the action continues, hidden from view.

Alix clearly uses this technique in Eustache's film in relation to the photograph *Vertigo*, named after the Alfred Hitchcock title and shown at the start of the short film – at this point the visuals and the discussion still match up with one another. The exchange with Boris Eustache helps to unravel part of the enigma of this photograph:

> BORIS: This photo is called *Vertigo*?
> ALIX: Yes, well this is called *Vertigo* for purely anecdotal reasons, because I saw *Vertigo* after taking this photograph; I mean the same afternoon. But anyway,

Vertigo le 14.VII.79 – *le* 14.XII.79

there isn't much of a connection; except I was suffering with quite severe dizziness while taking it. I had drunk a lot, this bottle was almost empty. Anyway, the story is very strange, the story of when this photograph was taken is quite odd.

BORIS: Do you want to tell me it?

ALIX: It is quite obscene. I was in an embarrassing situation with a friend. I lit a cigarette and he said to me, 'you're lighting a cigarette now, in these circumstances, like the whores in Amsterdam,' and I said, 'yes, why not. And not only can I light a cigarette, but I want to take a photograph.' And so I took this photograph. It was very hot, which I tried to show through this colouring, rather heavy-handed to be honest. But it just goes to show, a photograph can be personally pornographic while being publicly decent.

Alix smiles, amused, when replying to Boris's questions. She uses several euphemisms, not seeming to want to give too much away. The young man has to be persistent if he wants to solve the mystery of this picture. At first glance, the subject matter of *Vertigo* seems to be fairly tame and conventional, giving a view of Alix's apartment. Taken from the living room, it shows the door frame of the bedroom. A pair of women's shoes are lined up in the foreground. In the middle-distance, the centre of the photograph, there is an empty chair; on the right, a table on which stand a lamp, a teapot, some pieces of crockery, a bottle of alcohol and the cardboard box it was packaged in. The picture has been coloured with red and yellow pencils. It is a simple, reserved photograph. Yet Alix considered it to be pornographic. The viewer desperately tries to find a clue; suddenly the curves of the chair's backrest take on a sensual quality, the light grows intense, and the sandals appear to be the confession of a striptease. But the erotic nature of this print continues to elude us both in time and in the space it reveals. It was taken after sexual intercourse – which Alix refers to with false modesty as an 'embarrassing situation' accompanied by 'quite severe dizziness'; the instant at the origin of the picture is over. If we imagine time on a horizontal axis, the erotic moment that is the subject of the image is situated before it, to its left.

THE BACKGROUND of the photograph leads to the bedroom and the bed – part of the frame can be made out – but this part of the shot is overexposed: it is too white and deprives the viewer of the details. The lover must still be in the bed, but you can only see a dishevelled cover. Alix, who is taking the photograph, is also absent; the two protagonists are therefore concealed from us. In the film, explanations are only hinted at, and the picture becomes all the more intriguing as a result. The pleasure Alix tacitly refers to in Eustache's film has been hidden from view. *Vertigo* plays with the viewer; it deprives us of a subject and frustrates us by offering a space of perception that remains oblique.

The act of showing exists side by side with concealment, and the moment of intimacy is also one of exclusion. The frontality of the image reminds us of our status as viewer, imposing a distance: the object of desire, outside the frame, is denied us. The eroticism of Alix's photographic work, characterized by its mischievousness and yearning, thrives in an approach that plays on its shock value, or in absence and digression.

*

IN OCTOBER 1985, Claudine Brécourt-Villars published *Écrire d'amour* (*Writing on Love*), an anthology of erotic texts written by women, with Éditions Ramsay.

She invited Alix Cléo Roubaud to be part of the project, who contributed a text called 'Danielle Coloyan, User's Guide'. There are two versions of this text; the first was written in Alix's journal under the date 9 August 1979 – it therefore forms part of her private writing that has not been published; the second, later, version was published posthumously in *Écrire d'amour*. Along with a few letters, this is one of Alix's only erotic texts that remains.

DANIELLE COLOYAN
USER'S GUIDE
Alix Cléo Roubaud

DIRECTIONS OF USE

– traumatic pain: sprains, fractures, dislocations, postoperative pain.

Yes, you can take a Glifanan, it's good for mental pain. Mental, more expensive this year. In the taxi, twelve francs fifty plus the tip, from Saint-Germain to rue Vieille-du-Temple, a song, to be found.

In the taxi, an almost inaudible song plays on the radio. Can you turn it up? I love this song.

At my place (this is a romantic affair), some Boulaouane Vin Gris in the fridge, whisky, a mediocre white: you want white. And a Glifanan. No, nothing intravenous.

– Neurological pain: facial neuralgia

High cheekbones, etc. Crabby, indecisive, unwilling, she followed me almost by chance (this is a story). A Mogadon.

DOSAGE: DO NOT EXCEED TWO DOSES

a Mogadon. It will get you a little high, especially with what you are drinking. Partially undressed, very chic, naked: shaved armpits, waxed legs, trimmed hair, Helena-Rubinstein-painted toenails in trainers: ready for delivery, but already elsewhere. How I love this song, she says to me, and laughs out loud watching me go down on her because I am Canadian. Sleeping, talking, coming, maybe coming.

AVOID SIMULTANEOUS INTAKE OF
ALCOHOLIC BEVERAGES

maybe coming. More beautiful asleep, in her absolute absence, than awake in her intermittent absence.

SIDE EFFECTS

She is unemployed, like Marie-Laure, and Edith, and Jeanine. No, the Glifanan is not taken intravenously and if I were you I wouldn't mess around with that.

Dressed again, only talks to me about the song playing in the taxi, the one I don't know the name of, nor the words, nor the musicians, nor anything. Dressed: knickers, cotton shirt with turned down collar, navy blue aviator jacket.

Sings: I smoke because you drink, I drink because you smoke, etc., *da capo,* A, B, A', B. Preferably to be taken before meals. What's the thing you gave me called? MOGADON? and does it exist intravenously? because when you take things intravenously, that's how you really go that little bit further, you know.

   – chronic pain: visceral, dental, mental.

LOADING DOSE

   – I like her because I don't think she shows off.

   – What does that mean?

Because sentences that don't belong to her come out of her mouth; a stereotypy that is neither dental, lumbar, psychological, animal, grammatical, lexical, nor pharmacological. I, she, we, they are dispossessed of language

her inert body, pure figure of my secret expenditure. Body proper, proper noun: referring only to themselves, the body in sleep, the no in noun and non-sense. Proper; except this faint melody that may have penetrated the obscurity of her dreams, if she were dreaming at all.

Im   personal
       possible
       mediate
       lost.

                       playing to lose, making ends me.

Melancholy, more expensive this year.

                                            9.08.79

Breathing

You have difficulty breathing, yet your lungs are sound. Your bronchial tubes alone are afflicted with a condition that can often be cured and in all cases at least eased. It is essential to identify what that condition is and, therefore, to accept that you will have to go through some arduous periods, which will help you to better understand your body.

THESE ARE THE FIRST WORDS from a book on asthma, from the *Understand to Heal* series, found in Alix Cléo Roubaud's collection of books. Surprised by the presence of this well-being guide, I found it gave medical advice in a coaching style that combined therapeutic instructions, personal development tips and advice on nutrition. Alix seemed to be primarily interested in the 'Treatment' section, where she has filled the margins with the names of medications and their recommended dosages: '½ Ventoline', '1 Medrol, 3 times a day', 'Celestone'. Tucked in between the final pages, I found a leaflet on Bricanyl, a bronchodilator.

Alix suffered from chronic asthma. Bouts of bronchitis, spring allergies, coughs and breathing difficulties were her daily reality. She died of a pulmonary embolism. Her fragile health, which she did little to assuage (Alix smoked, drank alcohol, and sometimes used drugs), also imposed a sense of structure, demanding a regular schedule. Every year she followed a two-week course of treatment at La Bourboule, a thermal spa in the Monts Dore in central France. In August 1978, 1979, 1981 and 1982, Alix wrote letters and passages in her journal there. On 25 September 1978, Alix explained to her friend Anne, in a letter written in English:

> *Sécurité Sociale* (the French version of Medicare) sent me off to the mountains on a cure [...] a Magic Mountain quite devoid of intellectuals, but crammed with asthmatics of all sizes and shapes, avidly exchanging the more lurid aspects of their respective symptoms.

Dressed in linen, wearing a wide-brimmed hat, and reading Proust, Alix mocked the old-fashioned notion of the cure and announced, with amusement, that she was going to 'take the waters'.

She stayed there alone and devoted herself to the treatment.

> The doctor here had my whole file from Paris; I have been very well looked after; I have rarely recovered from a bronchitis flare-up so quickly and, in this case, it was bronchial pneumonia. Once my fever dropped, I resumed my treatment; I'm doing electro-aerosol therapy, inhalations and steam baths, after which, completely crimson (the thermal baths are 30°C, the thermal water 60°C), they entrust me to the care of a huge man with hairy arms, who lays me face down on a sort of table, hammers on my diaphragm, and pounds my sides until I cough.[14]

In the last years of her life the spa treatment was a ritual. It was a time of boredom and solitude. The isolation allowed her to take a step back from her life in Paris, and even if certain anxieties rose to the surface, illness was paradoxically no longer one of her struggles there. She wasn't eclipsed but objectified by the treatment. She was confronted with it every day and her symptoms grew less severe. Because her asthma, which took up all her days, was being taken care of, it was no longer a source of concern, but something simply to be acknowledged. In this setting she approached it from a scientific rather than a metaphysical viewpoint. La Bourboule was the time Alix took out of her life each year to breathe. She produced little, read a lot, and didn't speak. From these trips she drew the physical strength that allowed her to resume the course of her existence.

Beneath a strangely Byzantine dome, the thermal baths at La Bourboule form an imposing and calm monument. A large glass door opens onto the main hall, revealing smooth, shiny surfaces and arches that rise several dozen metres above the ground. The antique rose walls are punctuated by high windows that reveal stretches of sky. The signage hasn't changed since Alix's stay. Under the white interconnecting arches there is a sign that reads WOMEN'S INHALATION in gold capital letters and behind the counter at reception you find ELECTRO-AEROSOLS, NASAL IRRIGATION and GARGLES. The medical dimension of the setting is concealed behind a casual elegance. A round pool structures the heart of the main aisle, tall plants transform severity into sobriety, the hydrotherapy patients in their dressing gowns are quiet. The same cordial authority you would find in a mental health unit prevails in these baths. Everything is clean, the carers are attentive and smiling, the space is designed to encourage and organize the route the bathers take as they walk through it. The hall structures and clearly connects the different wings and functional spaces – TUBAL CATARRH, OTITIS and others. In the children's treatment room, toy building bricks and stickers of fluorescent fish are dotted about between inhalation devices and nasal douches. At the entrance to the adult area, a full-colour poster shows a delighted-looking family wearing bathrobes in front of the entrance to the building, under the slogan 'Bourboule, a unique city'. The remaining areas are only accessible to patients and doctors. They are tiled rooms brightened up with plastic chairs and signs displaying instructions like 'For the benefit of the treatment, please keep quiet to preserve the tranquillity of the room', 'avoid leaning forward and keep your head upright to facilitate the absorption of aerosols' and 'please do not read in this room (ink)'.

Sans titre (view of the main entrance to the Grand Thermes de La Bourboule), 1980.

Photographs taken by Alix at La Bourboule are rare. Documentary records for the most part, they offer an inventory of the different places she visited. A frontal view of the hall shows an open door towards the treatment areas. In the doorway three people are just visible in the surrounding white expanse. Some self-portraits were taken in a hotel room in La Bourboule, in which she poses completely naked, photographing her reflection in the mirror on a wardrobe door. These images are characterized by a sense of calm, their tones often muted. Breath is never their focus.

Alix's impeded respiration shaped her life. She was sometimes physically limited by her body, obliged to stay at home, medicate herself almost daily, and go for treatments. But this symptom also persisted in her work. In her journal, her prose is punctuated by intermittent blank spaces that give her sentences a jerky rhythm. Words collide where she didn't leave any space between punctuation signs, others are separated by irregular gaps. Alix left some passages gasping for breath, suffocated her writing. And this work of breath on the page drew on her asthma. Her style was constructed within a diagnosis and, at the same time, reached beyond it. Alix would later do the same with her photos.

In August 1980, when for the first time in several years she was not at the spa but in Saint-Félix with Jacques Roubaud, she created one of her most striking photographs: *Quinze minutes la nuit au rythme de la respiration.*

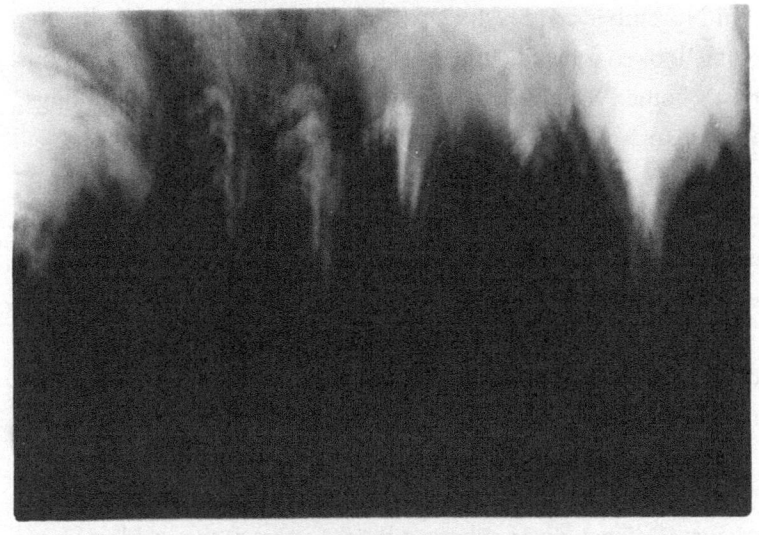

Quinze minutes la nuit au rythme de la respiration, 1980.

In this image no recognizable form can be made out, only simple black streaks topped with light, shivering halos. There is no line of perspective to give depth to the composition – it is a flat and abstract image. However, there's an immediate sense of familiarity to it. Behind this work – a sensitive palimpsest – looms another image, that of a radiograph.

The X-rays that enable radiological examination belong to the same physical family as light rays. They make an impression on radiographic film comparable to that made by light on photographic film. The fundamental difference is that X-rays penetrate the material – bones show up in white and the areas where there is air in black. The outlines are never sharp but appear almost blurred and slightly faded. *Quinze minutes la nuit au rythme de la respiration*, which presents the same tonalities, the same quivering contours, could also be a view of Alix's lungs saturated with air, or an enlargement of a tiny detail in her respiratory system. Then it would be a *photoradiograph*, the rewriting of an examination that Alix was frequently subjected to.

In November 2012, Alix's two small rooms on rue Vieille-du-Temple looked a bit like one of those reconstructions of a famous artist's home. When I first went in, Alix's papers, her belongings, the postcards pinned to the wall – everything was untouched. For a long time, I'd been searching for a place where we might coincide, a place where we could be present together in the world, despite her death. I thought I would find that in her apartment, but it felt deserted.

In a fleecy mass of dust gathered behind a radiator, I found a brown paper envelope from the angiology clinic in Aix-en-Provence. Inside were two X-ray images. The discovery came as a shock.

Even more so than the self-portraits, the nude photos and the texts, these images made me feel I had discovered something intimate. I'd been given what no longer existed: the inside of her body, her living matter, the contour of her flesh wrapped around bones. A photographic image only reproduces a surface which makes the best of loss. The photographic object is a platitude that feeds memory, centred, as it often is, on a fixed moment snatched from life. In these images of her there is a conflict: it is a medical image of a living body, but which brings to mind a ghost relating to the world through a layer of ectoplasm. And yet the first presupposition implied by the existence of such an object is life and what's more, in this case, respiration. Looking at this radiograph, I could see into Alix's body and her organs, I could see what was now definitively gone and the cause of her death. I was able to penetrate a lost density.

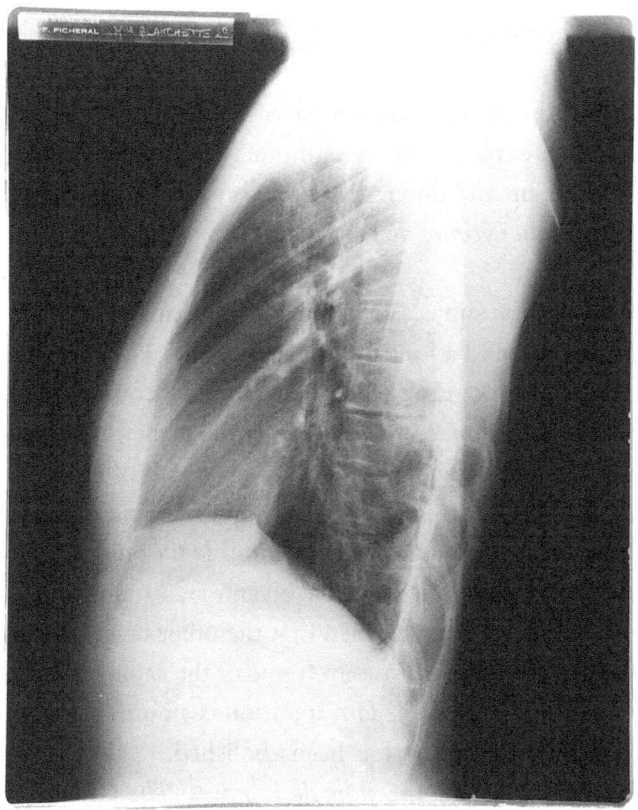

X-ray image of Alix Cléo Roubaud's lungs,
January 1975.

THE PREVALENCE of black in *Quinze minutes la nuit au rythme de la respiration*, just like in a radiograph, makes it resemble a negative at first glance. And if that's how we would describe the medical imaging used to show up all the details of the body, then *Quinze minutes la nuit au rythme de la respiration* is a positive. The qualities haven't been reversed, however. Two thirds of the image really are black. At first, this photograph looks like an X-ray image, and then it grows both technically and intrinsically distant from this likeness. This isn't a photograph of a respiratory system, but of breathing.

WHAT HAD ALIX chosen to photograph to achieve *Quinze minutes la nuit au rythme de la respiration*? On 20 November 1980, she wrote in her journal:

> Proof shot of the cypresses at St-Félix.Taken at night with an exposure of 10-15 minutes.Slight motion of the camera up and down due to my breathing.*quinze minutes la nuit au rythme de la respiration.*

She thus reveals the subject of the photograph and the way it was created: trees and a long exposure time. But I only really understood the photograph when I discovered a contact print abandoned in a cardboard folder. One of the vignettes showed a clear image of an ordinary landscape – a stretch of grass, a dirt track, a row of cypresses in the background, and the sky above them – the origin of *Quinze minutes la nuit au rythme de la respiration*. This was an objective inventory, a snapshot of a familiar panorama. I realized then that the other image, the smoky, non-figurative one, was a close-up frame of the same trees. *Quinze minutes la nuit au rythme de la respiration* is an unrecognizable landscape where all scenery has been abolished.

In his novel *Le Grand Incendie de Londres* (*The Great Fire of London*), Jacques Roubaud describes the circumstances in which the photo was taken. Alix was in Saint-Félix, above the house, in the vineyard. She was naked and she lay down on the ground in front of a row of cypresses. She chose an exposure time of a quarter of an hour and placed her camera on her chest, where it rose and fell with her breath. Her breathing made the trees shudder and infused the photograph with the movement that spreads through it from bottom to top. The black shadows and the grey wisps of smoke that they emit were her inhalations and exhalations. This is what makes *Quinze minutes la nuit au rythme de la respiration* a feat. Movement is captured without being fixed, it seems somehow to be enclosed in this shot and repeats itself *ad libitum*. The heart of the image beats forever, shifting with Alix's irregular breathing. It is a photograph of life itself. Worlds apart from the documentary-like shots taken at La Bourboule, *Quinze minutes la nuit au rythme de la respiration* is a self-portrait in breath.

THE TREES ALIX photographed in Saint-Félix are transformed by her body. An evergreen, the cypress is a symbol of eternity and the tree most often planted in cemeteries. I had a desire to see the cypresses of Saint-Félix again. I always said 'again' without thinking about it, until, surprised, I realized my mistake. Maybe because I knew them from *Quinze minutes la nuit au rythme de la respiration*, the reality of the cypresses seemed to ensue from the photograph. My trip to La Tuilerie de Saint-Félix marked the end of my quest. The only images I had of the place were those taken by Alix and so were deeply subjective. I used to imagine Pierre's workshop – which is what I still call it, using Alix's words, which grant me a familiarity with the unknown space through language – its rendered walls and paving stones underfoot, steps leading up to the main house, a huge hole in the wall photographed in *Le Baiser*, and a high copper bed in Jacques Roubaud's bedroom, where she photographed their siestas. Although this property belonged to the Roubaud family, through my research it had come to represent Alix more than it did Jacques. Like a synecdoche, or lieu de mémoire, for me it stood for her love for Jacques, her bouts of depression, her love of reading, her asthma and her talent as a photographer. Saint-Félix was *Si quelque chose noir*, *Le Baiser* and *Quinze minutes la nuit au rythme de la respiration*.

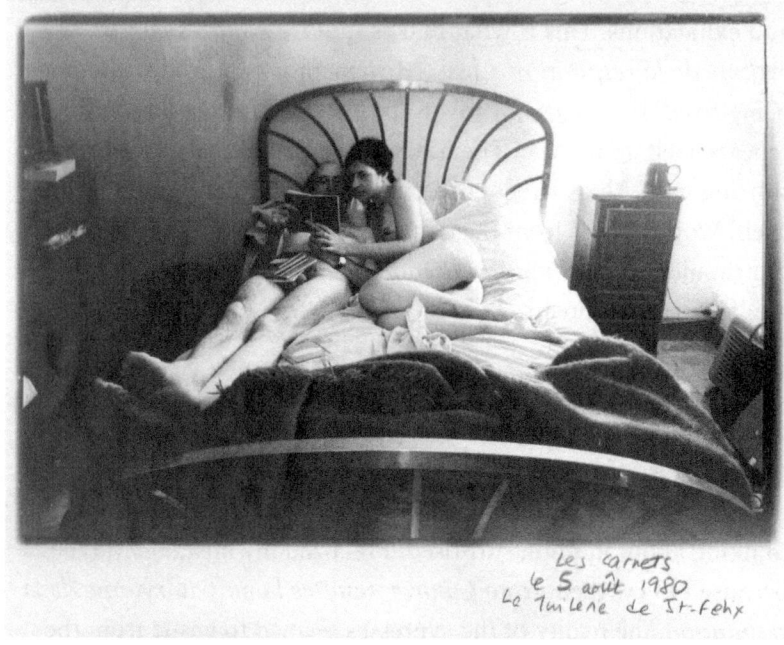

Les Carnets, le 5 août 1980 la Tuilerie de Saint-Félix
(Alix Cléo and Jacques Roubaud).

In Saint-Félix I found a vast plot of land dotted with buildings (two main houses) and surrounded by vineyards. The outer walls had the same even, brown curves sandwiched between the stone and grey mortar, the rounded, hollow tiles that give their character and name to La Tuilerie de Saint-Félix. The original activity – the manufacture of tiles – which had long since moved on from the inside of the building, still distinguished its outer facade. Pierre's workshop, where Alix created *Si quelque chose noir*, was enclosed by large, dusty shutters. In one of the houses, the bedroom she stayed in with Jacques Roubaud still appeared untouched, like the apartment on rue Vieille-du-Temple. When I arrived, I couldn't help checking – the copper bed, the books and the mirror that appear in her photographs had not been moved. I had followed the path of photography from its end to its beginning, coming to reality after the image, or more precisely, finding a reality produced by the image. The details of the architecture, the furniture and the natural surroundings emanate from the works of Alix. The materiality of the objects comes second, their origin being the fiction of the image. For me the primary existence of Saint-Félix is photographic.

DURING MY VISIT to La Tuilerie, *Quinze minutes la nuit au rythme de la respiration* was a persistent image. I wanted to see the trees that she photographed, to experience their existence. But when I looked at the row of cypresses, I didn't see *Quinze minutes la nuit au rythme de la respiration*. I wasn't there to prove a likeness between the two, but to confirm the power and illusion of the photograph. Standing among the vines where Alix had once stood, I thought back to her phrase: 'The photograph is not reality – it is much further away than reality.' The image stems from the tangible but radically transforms it. The majesty of these cypresses, all in all relatively common, highlights how innovative this photograph is: a landscape shaped by breath, a view unsettled by asthma.

If I wanted to see the cypresses again, it was to escape a feeling that time had stopped. Unlike Alix's apartment, the workshop, the places in general that I'd explored, and sometimes the people I'd met too, nature didn't appear untouched but permanent. Because they are evergreen – the cypresses are unlikely to fall in my lifetime – these trees were the place I'd been looking for where I might coincide with Alix. They persist outside Alix and me, bearing no trace of what has passed, and in this they bring us together. The cypresses, unchanged without being stilled, have that indifference which allows me to find a sense of time that feels true. At Saint-Félix I was able to calm an unchecked mysticism that had been troubling me.

While Alix's asthma is a biographical fact that can't be ignored, I must admit that I don't find myself fascinated by it. I believe, nevertheless, that *Quinze minutes la nuit au rythme de la respiration* is a remarkable creation. It condenses the train of thought necessary to understand her work. You have to go through the different stages of advanced commiseration – be saddened by her asthma, moved by the place, shaken by her death, and startled by the oracular feel of the pulmonary X-ray image. The inner drama is always alluring. Because Alix died young, was ill, and sometimes prone to depression, there is a temptation to read her work as completely autobiographical. It isn't. Her work was rooted in lived experience – a common practice – but she managed to extricate herself from those extreme states to offer something else. Alix moulded ideas that were uninfluenced by pathos, her personal life was only a starting point. *Quinze minutes la nuit au rythme de la respiration* is an expression of a conceptual approach, aimed towards finding an answer to the nagging question in photography: can the image diverge from the memory, its time be other than the past?

UNTANGLING THE LIFE from the work is a complex process. It is important to know that the cypresses and the asthma are a point of departure for understanding this work. Drawing on these two elements, Alix tried to make a photograph in the present. *Quinze minutes la nuit au rythme de la respiration* is a demonstration, Alix's twofold abolishment of the past. It is an abstract image, as the inability to recognize its subject prevents nostalgia. *Quinze minutes la nuit au rythme de la respiration* doesn't bear witness to any era gone by, since nothing is distinguishable in it. And it doesn't capture a moment but a duration. These are not moving images, but an image moved by the layering of the trees, veils of varying degrees of opacity governed by her exhalations. Like all the images of a film gathered into a single frame, or futurist paintings depicting speed, this photograph contains a movement that is endlessly relaunched. *Quinze minutes la nuit au rythme de la respiration* breaks the tautology of the image: it doesn't offer a mirror image of the world, instead eluding all resemblance. Like all of Alix's oeuvre, it is caught between a personal, intimate tendency – self-narration and self-portraiture – and a conceptual force – confrontation with the medium, the will to define something, and the primacy of the idea. You need to pass through La Bourboule, Saint-Félix and the illness, then put the story to one side at the threshold of the image before you enter it.

Si quelque chose noir

The series *Si quelque chose noir* is Alix's best-known work, if only by name. Jacques Roubaud's collection of poems, *Quelque chose noir*, creates an echo effect – the two titles are linked by their similarity and the meaning and connotations behind them. This series, which was exhibited in Arles in 1983,* is without doubt one of Alix's most accomplished. However, it is often misunderstood. The series is made up of a total of 17 photographs. This definitive number, chosen by Alix, is sometimes overlooked or unknown, so much so that *Si quelque chose noir* has almost never been reproduced in its entirety: only twelve photographs appear in the *Journal*, and not in the order she preferred them in. The Bibliothèque nationale de France is the only institution to own the full work. In addition to the 17 images, *Si quelque chose noir* includes, by way of an introduction, a photograph of a text written by Alix on her typewriter in July 1981. I have included this text along with five pictures from the series, those that are most often missing, in this fragment.

In 2010, the Centre international de poésie Marseille dedicated a publication to *Si quelque chose noir*. For the first time, all of the images were reproduced. They were printed on smooth, thick paper, numbered and arranged according to the artist's wishes.

---

*   The series was shown at the Rencontres d'Arles in 1983 (from 3 July to 30 September) at Galerie Arena. The group exhibition entitled *Les Gens de l'éphémère* (*Ephemeral People*) was conceived by Alain Desvergnes.

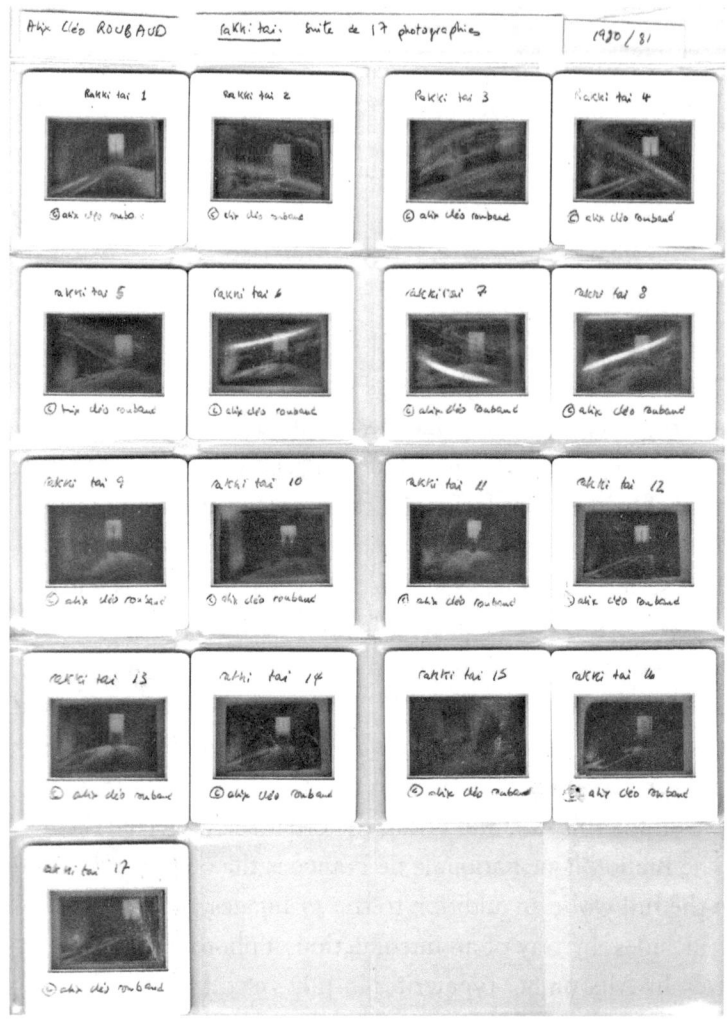

Slides of the series *Si quelque chose noir*, 1980-1981.

The publication of this book was possible because of a document that was found in the collection among the letters: slides of the series arranged in a plastic wallet. This is the only handwritten piece detailing the work, and has therefore served as a reference for cataloguing and showing *Si quelque chose noir*. Three strips of paper placed in horizontal slots at the top of the perforated, transparent sleeve show from left to right: 'Alix Cléo Roubaud', 'Rakki Tai: Sequence of 17 photographs' and '1980/81'. The writing on these strips, like on the white frames that surround the images, where Alix repeats the title and numbers them, has been done by hand. The slide film, which isn't protected but mounted in frames so it can be handled, is damaged: it is turning yellow and the surface is studded with dirt, dust and textile fibres, among other things.

THE STATUS of this document is paradoxical: although necessary for proper conservation and understanding of Alix's work, it breaks a fundamental rule. By enabling the images to be further developed and reprinted on paper, it allows for the creation of a posthumous work, which Alix was firmly opposed to. Looking at the original prints of *Si quelque chose noir*, with their richly varied and carefully worked shades of black, I know that the yellowing of these slides is not a desired effect, and that time has changed their colour. This set of slides constitutes a document rather than a work. It has the strange status of a secret: although the bearer of a truth, it must also be kept under wraps so as not to infringe on Alix's wishes.

Rakki tai – The Seated Demon

THE TITLE CHOSEN by Alix and written at the top of the document is 'Rakki tai', but the images are those of *Si quelque chose noir*. The series is also referred to in this way in the *Journal*. Jacques Roubaud has given an explanation for this dual designation: 'The first, abandoned title of her great sequence, *Si quelque chose noir*, had been *Rakki tai*, and *rakki tai* is one of the styles of medieval Japanese poetry, the "demon-quelling" style.' It was Jacques Roubaud who was first interested in this literary tradition and shared his research on the period with Alix. For Alix it was more a matter of inspiration than erudition. Without knowing all the nuances of the tradition, she adopted a principle inherent to *rakki tai*. It wasn't a question of Alix blindly giving in to the romantic notion of summoning demons.

RAKKI TAI appears for the first time in the writings of the great 13th-century poet Fujiwara Teika.* In the *Maigetsusho*, one of the poet's greatest works, Fujiwara Teika lists ten styles of poetry, building up to the pinnacle of the highest art of poetic composition. The first four styles, fundamental pillars, are the style of 'mystery and depth' (*yūgen*), the 'style of precise description' (*koto shikarubeki yō*), the 'splendid style' (*uruwashiki yō*) and the 'emotional style' (*ushin tei*). When learning to write poetry, once this foundation has been mastered, the five styles that follow are easy to tackle. Then comes the tenth and most difficult style: *rakki tai*. The complexity of *rakki tai* can be explained by the conflict between the fear inherent to the style – it is a matter of the poet measuring himself against elusive, malevolent powers – and the formal imperative which demands that each poem be elegant and delicate. Novices are therefore incapable of composing in this style; you must go through the first nine stages before coming to it.

Jacques Roubaud translates 'the demon-quelling style' into French as '*style pour dompter les démons*'. The verb 'quell', close to 'kill' in Old English, has quite a strong meaning: to subdue, extinguish, suppress. The English definition uses the term 'to beat down', which denotes violence combined with a downward movement. '*Dompter*', to subdue with force, to tame, is a subtle translation into French. The idea isn't the destruction of demons, but their bringing to heel. This expression is in keeping with what life is for each of us: it is rare to be able to completely eliminate that

---

* The scholarly research of two specialists, Robert H. Brower and Paul S. Atkins, helped me understand the origins and the meaning of *rakki tai*. I have used their English translations of the *Maigetsusho*.

which torments us, mastering it is doubtless the surest, clearest route to calm. Certain fundamental sources of anxiety cannot be wiped out but only dominated, perhaps. Our demons, inalienable possessions, must be commanded to be seated.

Si quelque chose noir 8/17, 1980-1981.

Dompter, I find this word troubling. We can tame rivers, skies, hearts or instincts; but more than the disciplining of the natural elements, the reduction of emotions to silence, or the subjugation of barbarians, for me the notion of taming immediately conjures up images of men confronting beasts, the glorious chariots of ancient Rome adorned with wild animals, an animal tamer face to face with a lion in an arena, circling the feline in an attempt to win it over and dominate it. Taming involves a body, a staging of this battle against the demons. Zeami, who was an actor, playwright and theorist of Japanese Noh theatre, adopted *rakki tai* and divided it into two sub-categories: the 'style of shattered movement' and the 'style of powerful movement'. The first style was linked to 'the form of a demon with a human heart' and therefore suggested a human body that was possessed; to convey this style actors had to contain the movement of their arms and legs. On the contrary, the second style involved violent, wild actions: you had to play the demon. Noh theatre gave flesh to the demonic force so that it could be laid low. *Si quelque chose noir* is a series composed of flesh: Alix is present in the 17 pictures, her naked body and its movements extending form and rhythm through the photographs.

IN THE SOMBRE SPACE of *Si quelque chose noir*, Alix tames while dancing, her body sketching an unrelenting choreography on the light-sensitive surface. She appears once, twice, even ten times in an image. The long exposure time allowed her to move around the workshop, making impressions in different places on the film. She also used double exposure to multiply her ghostly appearances. She explained the fundamental role of her moving body throughout the series in a letter:

> At the moment, I'm photographing myself in motion: I leave the shutter open for 10, 20, 30 seconds and I walk around in front of the camera: instead of picturing how my photographs will turn out, I do something like what action painters do but with my body. I started this work in Saint-Félix (where I had the wonderful space of Pierre's workshop) and now I'm beginning to understand a little bit about the speed needed for my movements to make an impression on the film. Therefore, I am my own paintbrush; and in fact, I have signed up for a dance class again, both to carry on this photography work accurately, and to manage my asthma.[15]

Si quelque chose noir is a ballet of *rakki tai*, but I don't know if Alix vanquishes a demon, if she is crossed by one, or if the enemy she struggles with is herself. Nevertheless, what Alix goes up against is unbeatable, because it is allied with death.

When I look at *Si quelque chose noir*, I see a bullfight, a photographic death dance. But Alix is both matador and bull, both the demon and its master, and the *muleta* she wields is the image, a lure for fear.

Si quelque chose noir 5/17, 1980-1981.

Si quelque chose noir stages the execution of the subject by the photographer, the death of Alix by her own hand. In the fifth picture, she appears four times in a diagonal strip of light: standing by the window, crouching down, lying on her front, supported by her elbows, then lying stretched out like a recumbent effigy. Her journey towards the tomb is broken down into regular intervals. Two lines of light form an oblique rectangle on the floor, a grave in which she slowly lies down. Playing out her death, photographing it, and discovering it after the event, Alix seemed to want to give herself an image of her own demise. She embodied the lure of suicide, the haunting demon she told of in the *Journal*, the one she came too close to. On 20 October 1981, she wrote: 'What does it mean to see yourself already dead? how can it be shown?' To tame is also to apprehend, to feel and experience so as to understand, to master. But what Alix wanted to see was impossible to simulate; death is not a demon.

Alix wanted to *project* her death with all the polysemic force of the verb: to place it in front of her, pre-empt it, and inscribe it on the surface of the film. But that could only be a senseless task. It is not possible to experience death. Life and death are mutually exclusive.

> Because life and death are no more symmetrically related than screen and image;you have to have lived to die;but blinded by life,we forget that we will die;and vice versa,death doesn't mean there has been life.
>
> I don't really know if death is a screen onto which I project and play over the film of my life,or if it is the image that hides from me the fact I am alive.Alive,I don't imagine myself dead;dead,I won't see life.But from closer up? how can you know? perhaps death is the folding of the one onto the other,the image of my future death projected onto the screen of my real death,or else hiding me? what? how can we imagine that death is not a projection folded over on itself in automorphism;like a slide of the Mona Lisa projected onto the Mona Lisa itself.[16]

Sometimes photography allowed Alix to turn away from the fact of annihilation, to capture it so she could distance herself from it more effectively. All taming implies proximity, a necessary confrontation. A remark from the journal resonates when I look at these pictures: 'Take photography seriously.So,no more death.' Photography is a conjuration.

Si quelque chose noir 16/17, 1980-1981.

Childhood makes an appearance in this dark lair. In three pictures, a smiling little girl sits beneath the window, with her head tilted to the side. Sometimes appearing translucent, at other times partly obscured by a black mark on the print, the little girl becomes a ghost. Her prettiness is incongruous next to Alix's corpse stretched out on the stone floor. I came across this child again in Alix's apartment, painted by her mother Marcelle on canvas. She is identical to the girl in the photograph, with the same pose, rounded cheeks, and a white bow in her hair. It is a picture of Alix as a child, taken in Egypt – a family photograph.

Continued the *atelier* series,
      myself as a laughing child in
      front of my dead body.

This apparition changes the meaning of *Si quelque chose noir*: Alix isn't just working on a staging of death, but also on the cycle of life. The series is an example of satori, a reflection on the tenuous nature of human existence. This is where a poetic form comes in, in addition to the style of *rakki tai*: the haiku. These short poems, derived from the tanka, comprise 17 syllables (5/7/5). The number 17 that links the series and the haiku was not picked by chance and, like the poetic form, *Si quelque chose noir* allows life to emerge just as it is. The series might be thought of as a loop circling from the child to the corpse.

Si quelque chose noir 12/17, 1980-1981.

Variations on Black

AFTER ALIX'S DEATH, Jacques Roubaud adopted the title of the series for his elegiac collection *Quelque chose noir*, removing the 'if'. Death does not deal in hypotheticals; it cannot be challenged. What was an attempt – a question – becomes fact. Jacques Roubaud has explained that 'some thing black' is an ungrammatical expression that relates to the feeling of ruin brought about by death. For him, black becomes a verb.

How did Alix come to choose this title in the first place? There is no conclusion, the sentence is left hanging, unfinished. I ask myself, *If some thing black*, and then what? The conditional floats, unattached to a main clause. The base of the sentence is missing. Perhaps the photographs are the second part of the statement, an apodosis in image form. Or should it just be, *If some thing black*, then nothing?

BLACK, A SYMBOL of mourning and despair, absorbs rays of light, representing the dissolution of the visible spectrum, an absence of colour, but it is also the very substance of photography. As the shade of tragedy, it lends itself to a depiction of demons yet to be tamed, those that bring darkness with them. But more fundamentally, black prompts us to think about the notion of the image. In Alix's title, the word appears in place of a verb. Black is an action. And in fact, what is photography if not the production of black, the darkening of silver salts? In etymological terms, photography is writing with light, but it produces black. The chemical reaction that makes it possible to extract darkness from light is the very condition of photography.

Si quelque chose noir 14/17, 1980-1981.

THE FOURTEENTH PHOTOGRAPH in the series is taken from the same shot as the sixteenth. Alix lies between two streams of light on the right-hand side, and a little girl sits beneath the window, an unchanging, central point in the image. Image 16/17 is underexposed, darker, distinguishable by the density of blacks. The light in it is less blinding and the shadows carving out the shape of the body are more precise, giving Alix the appearance of a sculpture. But the vital difference is that in photograph 14/17 a black strip comes into the image from the left, like the rotations of a slide viewer switching from one image to the next. The encroaching black space threatens this photograph with obliteration. While the strip on the left side is underexposed, the right part of the image is slightly burnt: the two spaces represent two different exposures of the same photograph. Light is essential in the creation of an image, and it can be a threat. When exposed to the sun's rays for too long, a photograph fades into white, but deprived of light, it sinks into black.

In the Alix Cléo Roubaud collection there are pictures from *Si quelque chose noir* that went wrong or have been damaged. Some are faded from being exposed for too long, others are covered with yellow stains because of a fault with the fixer. These photographs that will never be exhibited show the immense work put in by Alix to get to the final prints. The discarded copies that are in the collection are precious because they uncover a process: an artwork is formed from trials, failures and adjustments. The medium too must be tamed.

EVEN THE MOST beautiful prints – with careful washing and optimal conservation conditions – can never be frozen in time. The chemistry that brought them into being continues its slow advance. The picture will be destroyed by what created it. Alix's works are particularly fragile. I can tell that some have aged since the shooting of Eustache's film, their features gradually transformed. The finite life of a photograph gives it a future, and a fate.

Trial for *Si quelque chose noir*, 1980-1981.

Sequences

IN 1982, Alix was selected to participate in a group exhibition at the Maison des arts André-Malraux in Créteil. She showed *Si quelque chose noir*. A photograph of her posing next to the series shows the work hanging in the gallery.

ALL OF THE PICTURES apart from the first were displayed in pairs, mounted on a rectangular piece of white cardboard. The mounts were lined up with no space left between them. *Si quelque chose noir* is an ordered series, a sequence. But unlike in film, where shots follow one another and merge, the photographs remain distinct entities. A photographic sequence is made up of separate, still images. Alix focused on this fact in *Si quelque chose noir* and decided to reveal the black frame surrounding each shot. The text written to introduce the series is dedicated to this enduring limit between the images:

> Sur la pellicule, les images se suivent sans se toucher. C'est
> la barre qui les sépare que nous regardons ici, tâchant de mettre
> cet invisible bord au centre de notre propos, de faire de la limite
> d'une image son sujet.
>
> Nous avons travaillé à la barre, comme les danseurs, nous y pliant,
> pivotant autour d'elle, afin de nous y faire. Etrange gymnastique
> que ce travail à la barre; là où nous voulions déplacer une frontière,
> c'est elle qui nous a déplacé. Car déplacer une frontière, c'est
> occuper un territoire; mais cette conquête n'a été que reddition:
> La barre est une évidence de la pellicule, évidence à laquelle
> il faut se soumettre.
>
> Suivons, station par station, la traversée de l'image par la barre;
> portons son poids, levons sa cruciforme et crucifiante difficulté.
> L'image n'est guère moins lourde que ce qui l'enferme.
>
> Paris, juillet 1981
>
> *ALIX CLEO ROUBAUD*

Si quelque chose noir,
introductory text, 1980-1981.

On the film the images follow one another without touching. It is the vertical part of the frame separating them that we are looking at here, trying to put this invisible boundary at the centre of our intention, to make the boundary of an image its subject.

We have worked at the limit point, like dancers, bending and pivoting around a barre, to reconcile ourselves to it. This dance is a strange form of gymnastics; where we wanted to move a boundary, it moves us. Because to move a boundary is to occupy a territory; but this conquest was nothing more than a surrender: the boundary is a fact of the film, a fact we must submit to.

Let's follow the boundary on its trajectory as it crosses the image; let's support its weight, its cruciform and crucifying difficulty. The image is no less heavy than that which contains it.

Alix Cléo Roubaud at the exhibition
Une autre photographie, Maison des arts
André-Malraux, 1982.

Alix introduces *Si quelque chose noir* as an impossible battle against photography. The film marks out the boundaries of each image, there is no getting past it. It is not a succession but a series which divides time into separate instants. And this understanding of the image is also the subject of *Si quelque chose noir*. The material photographic object cannot be tamed.

*

THE CATALOGUE number of Alix's photographs held in the collections at the Bibliothèque nationale de France is 'EP 5000'. The curators had reserved this number for a special bequest, to give it symbolic significance in the archive.

The Institution

From 1980, Alix became determined to establish herself as an artist. She gradually gave up on her thesis and stepped up her photographic work. However, the long hours she spent in the darkroom were no longer enough. For the photographs to have a life of their own, they needed to be brought to an audience. She approached a number of galleries, sent off portfolios for exhibitions and grants, but the responses were negative. Alix died having only once exhibited her work, without benefiting from the success of her exhibition in Arles. It took 25 years for her pictures to garner interest, for them to be welcomed by the institution.

ALIX WANTED her pictures to be seen and also wanted to sell some of her prints. In 1979, she chose to show them at her home, simply pinned up on her living room wall:

> I hold viewings on the first Wednesday of every month, where I put my latest photos up on the wall, and since August alone this single initiative has brought me enough people and recognition.[17]

For these soirées, which were both private exhibitions and an opportunity to meet people, Alix sent out invitations in the form of proof prints of her photographs with a few words written on the back. All those close to her have kept copies of these cards. It

FRONT: *La Cuillère*, Saint-Félix, 1980.
REVERSE: invitation addressed to Martine Broda,
Wednesday 4 March 1981, not sent.

didn't take long for her to sell a few prints, and she took on the task of showing new photographs every month.

Alix handled her pictures with limited care; some prints are covered in textile fibres, others that have been pulled from their mounts are torn or have remnants of brown sticky tape on them. Some of the prints displayed at her monthly soirées still have pin marks through them.

IN 2012, nearly 30 years after her death, the Centre Georges-Pompidou hung 13 of Alix's photographs in its permanent exhibition space. Displayed in clear frames on white walls, accompanied by immaculate exhibition signage, and curated in such a way that the pictures resonated subtly with one another, this presentation was a world apart from those evenings held on rue Vieille-du-Temple.

It was not so much the quality of the display material that mattered, but the new status that the museum bestowed on the images. By dedicating its walls to Alix's photographs, the Centre Georges-Pompidou endowed them with two new qualities: independence and legitimacy. Her work stands on its own, worthy of its place on the museum walls, where it contends with the other items in the collections. On display for visitors to see, Alix's pictures tell us that the stories and justifications are no longer necessary. Within the confines of these walls they have earned a right, a value. The institution cut the circumstantial ties linking Alix's work to that of Jacques Roubaud. The relevance of these images no longer needs to be proved. Once in the museum, the photographs have acquired the status of artworks.

HOWEVER, MUSEUMS also take away, selecting only the very essence of the work, the best pictures. The role of museums is to dazzle and captivate us, but what should I do with the parts of the collection that remain once the most spectacular pieces have been taken out of it? In earning a status, the pictures lose something of their human quality, the sense of the craft – the making – that has gone into each one. The collection is cleansed of its failed takes.

After dropping the photographs off at the Centre Georges-Pompidou, I went back to help with the captioning and to clarify some of the dates. I remember going through the basement rooms of this great art machine. In the room where the works were held, controlled low temperature, bright light and white gloves were de rigueur. After spending decades in the possession of her loved ones, then being sorted and classified at my home, the photographs were in a transitional space here, a sort of antechamber to knowledge. They were cleaned, examined in detail, and given the specialist care they required, after being neglected and handled by amateurs for so long.

Once an artwork becomes part of the collections, it must be named. This is where cataloguing comes in, which describes each photograph in detail and matches it up with various categories and standards. The librarians at the Bibliothèque nationale de France carry out this meticulous classification work on a daily basis, one of the most visually demanding exercises I have ever experienced. Dozens of questions come up for each piece: in the aesthetics section, should I note 'shadow effects' or 'lighting effects'? What term should be used to indicate a mark on the print? What genre of image is it? For example, 'interior', 'nude', 'landscape' or 'still life'? It is rare to be able to spend several minutes like this in front of a single work, questioning its every detail. Some of Alix's pictures were more difficult to classify than others. One of them was particularly complex.

Two men dressed in black appear to the right of a fractured space. Above them, a mirror whose frame has been enhanced with black pen reveals part of a room and the reflection of a woman sitting slightly hunched over. I had to authenticate the source of this photograph to fully appreciate Alix's use of appropriation and

Sans titre, circa 1980.

to be able to include it in the record of the work. This is a portrait of Auguste Renoir and Stéphane Mallarmé taken by Edgar Degas. The history of art and photography at play in this image are vital to understanding it, and the keys to this knowledge must be passed on to viewers of the picture. Research is composed of a series of breakthroughs or advances, but we need to establish a starting point.

THE LANGUAGE of the archive is a mix of precision and poetry. I was delighted by the concept of a 'subject search term', which makes it possible to highlight an object that appears in a photograph in a given record. Visitors searching the BnF catalogue can then find all the images featuring, for example, a cat, a chair, or a hat. When it came to one of Alix's portraits of Eustache in which the director is smoking and holding a telephone handset, I wondered whether to note 'cigarette' or 'telephone'. The categories raise fundamental questions about the picture. Because the telephone was integral to the relationship between Alix and Eustache, I decided to go with that. The clarity necessary for each record prevents an accumulation of these subject search terms; ideally there should only be one, a choice needs to be made. As precise and methodical as the archive may be, it also bears the traces of the person who created it, the unknown individual who prefers telephone to cigarette, who notices the light more than the darkness. A space persists and, on rare occasion, the eyes of the individual might not settle on the most accurate choice.

The photographs must go through this rigorous inspection before reaching the picture rails of the exhibition room. Some of the details gathered – artist's name, title, date, materials – are used to write the museum labels, a more formal, thorough introduction to the works than that offered by Alix in her apartment. There is a healthy sense of modesty in the work of the archive; both meticulous and anonymous, its primary function is to pass on information. Referencing allows documents to be found and knowledge to be circulated. The person searching a catalogue, whether a curator or a reader, is the main concern of the cataloguer, who themselves are never named. The archive is a kind of gift.

ONE OF THE INSTITUTION'S aims is to conserve works of art, and so we are kept at a distance, separated by the glass of the frame, and weighed down by the sense of authority it imposes. If a picture is directly handled, it will eventually be damaged. It is a paradox of conservation that a work is suspended beyond our reach to ensure its existence. At the centre of the painstaking work of conservation is the object, but a photograph is so much more than this flat, fragile materiality.

Restoration teams sometimes forbid the exhibition of certain works. Their lifespan is extended by keeping them in darkness.

I like to give art objects a little space in which to emerge, to flourish. For months, I opened my apartment to artists, researchers, curators and those who were simply curious, to show them Alix's photographs. All I had were some gloves and a few cardboard boxes. The pictures were sometimes touched and handled directly. Holding a work of art in your hands allows you to say something different about it. I adored this time when the photographs were a living entity, shared by all who desired to see them. In those days, the pictures were seen in their unembellished simplicity, they hadn't yet been attached to a name and a place. But that couldn't last forever. I strove so that the museum would protect Alix's work. And by embracing this collection, the institution is giving it back to us as a work of art. She smashed through all the anecdotal perceptions of her. And just like that, Alix was stripped of her mistakes and imperfections. She became an artist according to a well-established formula: fresh, innovative perspective, theoretical depth, chaotic life. And if you see these small selections of ten to 30 pictures, you think all her photographs are equally stunning. That's when they suddenly close themselves off to us, and we disconnect, because we still have to try, try again, fail.

THE DONATIONS to museums meant letting go: Jacques Roubaud parted with his wife's works, I gave up pictures that I had taken care of for years. When I began my work, I realized that I would sometimes say 'my photos', even though I had never thought of myself as their author or owner. A sense of familiarity – intimacy – had grown in me and I needed to shake it off. The archive, the institution allowed me to do that, to tell myself again and again, I am just a moment, the pieces will still exist, and all the more so, when others take charge of them. Relieved to pass them on, I began to write 'the photographs'.

The Thing That's Missing

I HAD THOUGHT I would be able to understand everything, meticulously piece together a life and unravel the mystery of a body of work, while making room for the trial runs and failed attempts; faced with all this, the absence would have faded. But I gave up. It was impossible to be exhaustive: the first chapters of her thesis were nowhere to be found, her camera lost, documents from before 1979 scarce, her book collection incomplete, and her journal under seal, published in a truncated version. And knowing whether Alix was haughty, kind, or passionate was of little concern to me. I don't take much interest in psychological approaches that treat artwork as a symptom. So, some mysteries remain; that of her death is paradoxically the most enduring. The doctor who certified the death concluded that the cause was a pulmonary embolism, others talked of suicide. Two people also claimed that doctors had diagnosed Alix with Hodgkin's lymphoma. The last pages of her journal, where Alix mentioned a 'fatal illness' and described undergoing medical tests, may corroborate this version of events. Personally, I don't consider her death to be an enigma. Detailing the causes of death won't change what happened.

THE THING that's missing, and I'm still looking, is not biographical but documentary in nature. The Alix Cléo Roubaud collection suffers from a significant shortfall: apart from

Eustache's film, we have no sound recordings. Alix listened to a lot of music and spoke about it, but the compilations she recorded for loved ones have never been found. In letters she wrote, Alix mentioned her interest in minimal music – she attended a Philip Glass concert in 1978 – which aligned with her research on Ludwig Wittgenstein and Gertrude Stein. In the apartment on rue Vieille-du-Temple, there was a Schönberg record – the master of the twelve-tone technique – among her philosophy books. The composer's apprentice, John Cage, is cited a number of times in Alix's texts. The fundamental principles of atonality – interval and serialism – are also leitmotifs in Alix's works. But none of her writings establishes an explicit link between music, philosophy and photography.

ALIX WAS A FRIEND of the composer and conductor Carman Moore. They kept up a correspondence from 1970 to 1980. Carman Moore went on to enjoy an international career working with some of the world's greatest names, including Pierre Boulez, Seiji Ozawa and Isaiah Jackson. During a number of trips to the United States – her father was appointed ambassador to the Organization of American States in Washington, D.C. between 1976 and 1980 – Alix met this musician friend and discovered jazz. In 1976, she wrote to a close friend (whom she inexplicably called '*chou-rave*' – 'kohlrabi' in English – which makes it difficult to identify him) back in Canada about her recent stay in New York and the clubs she went to:

> Anyway, I managed to see Jaki Byard and Bobby Hutcherson, the Rashied Ali Quintet (with Don Pullen on the piano, in a club where I offered Frank Wright a drink before realizing that he was already completely wasted), a Richard Clay Quintet (? never heard of him) with Walter Davis on the piano and Richard Davis playing the bass.

The artists mentioned played free jazz and belonged to the musical avant-garde of the 1970s. Alix's knowledge on the subject was therefore fairly comprehensive. In Alix's apartment, I found some jazz vinyl, including records by Keith Jarrett, Wayne Shorter – one of her favourite musicians, her German lover told me during our interview – Gary Burton and Bill Evans, and classical music (from Beethoven to Purcell, via Wagner and Bartók). With what I know, I can map out a summary of her musical tastes, but I'm not able to hear her voice.

ALIX WAS profoundly interested in sound, whether melodic, contemporary, or spoken. In 1979, she dreamed of buying a Nagra tape recorder, but her finances at the time couldn't stretch to one. Towards the end of her life, she began recording radio dramas. She had thought up a crime fiction piece with a friend, François B. On 10 July 1982, she described this new project to her mother:

> My friend, François B., who has worked in town planning for years and dreamed of doing something more fun, suggested we start working together on a crime series for the radio, because his best friend runs the only *radio libre* channel* that pays well in Paris and they're looking for ideas... So we have been playing around with tape recorders and we already have an hour's worth of a sketch on cassette, and I must say we have such a good time doing it (over the last year I must have read a hundred detective novels, which just goes to show that nothing is a waste of time). We are <u>inventing</u> a detective story, which is more fun than adapting one; we are

---

* *Translator's note*: *Radio libre* channels were clandestine pirate stations until the state monopoly on radio broadcasting was abolished following the election of François Mitterand in 1981. After a law passed on 29 July 1982, they were allowed to broadcast, but were expected to remain non-commercial.

working with two voices; but you can create a whole world with two voices and two basic tape recorders if you use your imagination.

These stories must have been broadcast on Radio Nova, a Parisian station created in 1981 that played non-mainstream music, but Alix died before she was able to finish them. Making the most of a new recording device she had purchased, she also produced short one-minute sequences: '27 October 1982: I'm working on the tape recorder (some very short prose pieces on sleep)'. The cassettes and tape recorders have not been found. François B. and Alix's brother didn't keep any copies.

FRIENDS AND FAMILY had spoken to me about Alix's 'very 19th-century' aristocratic diction. In *Les Photos d'Alix*, the inflections in her voice were distinctive, but the short film's 19 minutes are not enough to really hear it, and I can barely remember her conversation with Eustache, which I heard just once in 2010. Alix's intonation never ceases to surprise me: it is familiar to me from the dialogue in Eustache's film, but I wouldn't be able to recognize her voice in other situations. The pictures and the texts remain, but the sound of her voice is gone. Simple, immediate objects, such as a notebook or a photograph, are better able to stand the test of time. Technology is transient; constantly moving forward, it leaves behind its beginnings, rendering obsolete all that has come before it. The anonymity of a cassette, a tape recorder, means they are not automatically considered to be works of art. Their banality makes them easily accessible, and means we are less careful handling them, but in reality, these items are fragile. I imagine they were probably thrown away, or maybe they were put somewhere out of the way, because they had become obsolete, forgotten at the bottom of a drawer.

Unlike its content, which must be contained and defined, and its subject, which is often dead, the archive is very much alive and never ends. It will always be possible to add a new section to the Alix Cléo Roubaud collection if, for example, these recordings turn up. To me, the work in the archive seems infinite: there could be more documents, and the research could be refined by delving further into the artworks, grasping their subtleties, and exploring their impact. The progress I set in motion has gone beyond me; this would be the work of a lifetime, or of several.

Le Baiser

In august 1980, Alix spent two weeks in Saint-Félix. I found images on a contact sheet which she had taken at the time and never printed. They included pictures of Alix relaxed and naked in the garden, lounging in the sun. Jacques Roubaud looks on, always in the background, dressed, and in the shade. It is the afternoon and Alix's revelling in her eroticism sets up a contrast: the serious poet, with his polo shirt buttoned to the top and his legs crossed, sits opposite Alix, a reckless pleasure-seeker.

Sans titre (Alix Cléo and Jacques Roubaud),
detail from a contact sheet, Saint-Félix, 1980.

Alix let herself drift with the free-floating time of the holidays. She photographed erotic siestas, the light, the solid, quiet interior of the house, Jacques Roubaud standing in the alley of cypresses. But it was also a dark time, caught between between two suicide attempts: she swallowed sleeping pills on 14 August and again on 20 August. She was saved at the very last moment by those close to her. Death is omnipresent in the *Journal* entries from August 1980, and it seemed inevitable to her. It was around this time that she staged her own death in her photograph series *Si quelque chose noir*.

One photograph taken during this period particularly stands out to me: *Le Baiser*. It links death and love, and is reminiscent of a line written in her notebook in Saint-Félix, a few days after her suicide attempt: 'terrified of beginning the agony all over o it was o so easy with you here.' As though this peaceful existence with her husband, in the family home, made death possible, enabled Alix to do the inevitable, but without the terror.

Fig. 1: *Le Baiser*, Saint-Félix, 1980.

In *Le Baiser*, Alix and Jacques Roubaud are entwined. He has his back to the camera – you can only see the back of his head and the upper part of his torso. Almost completely hidden behind him, we imagine Alix facing him, her mouth against his. She pulls him towards her: one hand, placed on the nape of her husband's neck, seems to want to fuse their two faces. They are kissing. Alix and Jacques are standing in front of a stone wall, which has an oval-shaped hole in it. Jacques's left shoulder is blocking part of this black ellipse (originally a bread oven). There are many prints of this image, with slight adjustments in the densities: Alix produced lighter and darker versions of this kiss.

These variations orchestrated in the darkroom change the image. In the darkest and perhaps definitive version (Fig. 2) – Alix printed it on beautiful, thick baryta paper, which brings out the shades of black – Roubaud's shirt is almost indistinguishable from the cavity in the wall. A funereal gloom spreads from the opening and proliferates throughout the image, swallowing the bodies, and

Fig 2: *Le Baiser*, Saint-Félix, 1980.

leaving only the areas of bare skin untouched. And Alix, invisible, hidden by her husband's silhouette, seems to extend this dark flaw: the oval shape created by the bend in her arm mirrors it perfectly. She continues it and embodies it; she is this blackness which pulls Jacques Roubaud towards her. It is a terrible and romantic image: woman as death, temptress and femme fatale; the kiss of the Sphinx. By dabbling in chemistry, Alix stained the meaning of this kiss. As the shades of black deepen, she no longer embraces her husband but clasps him tightly, she is no longer protected by the beloved body but lies in wait behind it. She is a black hole that consumes everything.

This image, at first sight one of love, becomes unsettling the more closely it is studied. Why does it show this woman without a face? What is the meaning of this strange position? Not knowing exactly why I felt uneasy about it, I scrutinized the picture, expecting something to emerge. The hands, which I examined endlessly, and which give rhythm to the composition, are strange: one of them, very expressive, is placed on the beloved's head and the other, by his neck, creates three creases in the fabric of his shirt. The two prints can be distinguished not only by their different levels of contrast, but also by their framing (closer or more distant) and a slight adjustment of the position of the hands. In the first photograph (Fig. 1) they are touching, the thumb of one hand brushing against the little finger of the other, and they are distinctly placed on Jacques Roubaud's body. In the second (Fig. 2), more dramatic image, one of the hands is caught up in his hair and is partially covered by it. The saturation creates a clean cut between the light skin of the fingers and the brown of his hair. And spending a lot of time looking at this hand, I was gripped by a hallucination. It is not a caress. Alix is sinking her fingers into Jacques Roubaud's skull.

BUT THAT WASN'T ALL. I still couldn't see what was bothering me about *Le Baiser*. I don't think that it necessarily had anything to do with the 'unsayable' in photography, but rather that my eye was missing something.

WHEN I FINALLY saw why I was struggling with this picture, the detail that I discovered changed everything: the hands don't match. One belongs not to Alix but to Jacques Roubaud, who contorts his body to be able to reach the nape of his own neck. Looking more closely, my intuition is confirmed: the nails are thicker, the knuckles hairy. Doubled hands make two bodies that cannot be untangled. He, she, the void become one.

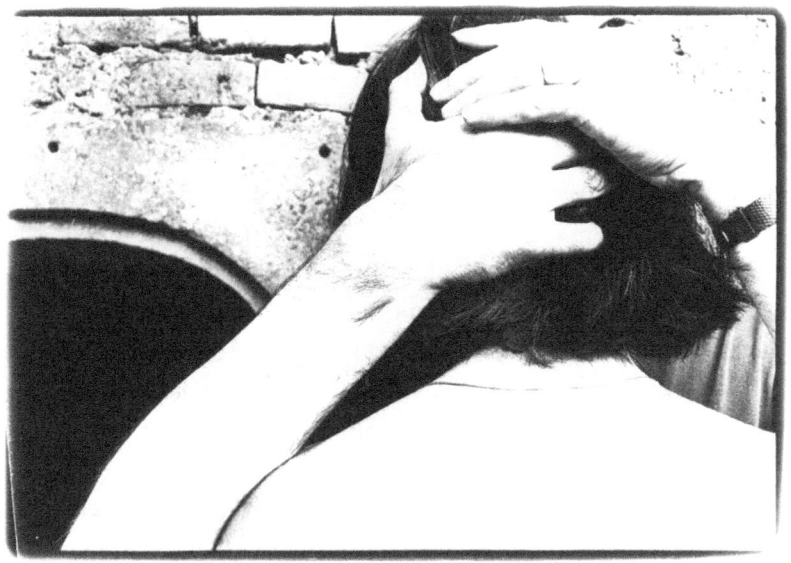

Fig 3: *Le Baiser*, Saint-Félix, 1980.

In another iteration of *Le Baiser* (Fig. 3), Alix has reversed the roles: this time she offers her back to the camera. This is a light picture, a little overexposed: the skin tones are dazzlingly bright, which has smoothed out any imperfections. She is seen from behind, her dark black hair cut in a bob. A line around the base of her neck marks out the neckline of her top, or perhaps a necklace against her bare skin. Two arms, the same this time, both belonging to Jacques Roubaud, pull her to him. On the right, his hand looks strangely similar to the one in the first version of the image, wearing the same ring and watch strap. The picture is one of sharp contrast: there is very little grey, and an almost blinding white. The framing is different – much tighter – you can now see the shoulders and not the back, the top of Alix's head is cut off, and the elbows are outside the camera's range. Only the upper right-hand quarter of the bread oven is visible, and in such a way that the effect of perspective seen in the other shots is cancelled out in this case. This is a much flatter picture than the first. And Alix's thick hair, a new echoing of the dark hole, appears pressed up against the wall. Jacques Roubaud can barely be seen: an opaque shadow surrounds his right arm on both sides, his chest is completely engulfed, and the light coming into the image from the right-hand side dissolves the rest.

ONCE AGAIN, Alix doesn't allow herself to be embraced, cornering him instead. This is another disconcerting picture: Jacques Roubaud's almost solarized forearm, bizarrely skewed by the lack of depth, looks like it has been cut out, leaving only the outlines. And against the top right-hand edge of the print, emerging from Alix's hair, you can see an eye, an evenly veiled crack, which merges with the pattern of joints in the stonework. Once you have seen the eye, which is just a small detail in the image, it becomes persistent: a lone pupil floating independently of any human face, staring at us. I see it as a voiceless appeal, which changes everything. He is no longer pulling her towards him but trying to tear himself away from her. This cyclopean eye is the only remaining part of him that she hasn't swallowed, the last thing stopping him from disappearing completely into the shadows.

FOR *Le Baiser*, Alix chose the framing, positioned the camera on a stand, and worked out their poses, but she didn't press the shutter. She asked her brother-in-law, Pierre Getzler, to take this picture that she had thought up and composed. This meant she also asked him to watch and to take part. A terrible event is played out in this photograph, one that would be repeated that summer in Saint-Félix. Alix offers Jacques Roubaud an experience of death. She invites him to contemplate her death; a cruel offer which reminds me of the final picture of *Si quelque chose noir*. Jacques Roubaud is lying on the ground, and Alix is lying on top of him. They are naked and she touches his face with one hand. But while he appears clearly, she is already fading, a translucent shadow that has, in places, disappeared completely from view.

Si quelque chose noir 17/17, Saint-Félix, 1980.

The eye belongs to the person bearing witness. In *Le Baiser*, the witness is the husband who is first asked to take part in the staging of an ambivalent love scene, and then confronted with a sinister black hole that erases them both by turns. Jacques Roubaud sees himself twice: first standing in the pose and then, once the photograph has been developed, from within the scene pictured in it, through his single eye. How can we not think of death, so present for Alix and brushed against during this trip to Saint-Félix, when we read these words from the *Journal*: 'You will see me dead Jacques Roubaud'? But Jacques Roubaud – the witness – does not have to testify, as this scene plays out in the fictional space of the photograph. He is a nonsensical observer who has been asked to corroborate the truth of a fantasy – it is a paradoxical demand. And yet, this potentiality, that of the dead woman and her survivor, the onlooker and death, will be realized. Alix delivered proof of the future to come.

(BLACK)

Chiswick, 1980.

Let's pull the cord, hide this last photograph from view. I'll leave Alix's memory there. I wanted to write between the pieces of evidence. An account has emerged. Memories are words, and archives are documents.

Fleshing Alix out in fiction was not my intention; I worked in the interstices between the traces of her that remain.

This is not a photograph of Alix's life, but fragments of her work; scattered shards.

A picture that may be true.

Coda

JACQUES ROUBAUD

Afterword

I

IN THE LAST days of August 1979, around 41 months before her death, Alix made two decisions. The first was to dedicate herself exclusively to one thing going forwards, photography. Her sole aim would be to be a photographer, or rather, more precisely, to become a photographer, in the sense she gave to the word. She wanted to be able to say, 'I'm a photographer', like you say, 'I'm a poet', or 'I'm a mathematician'.

The first decision, that of giving up all her other activities and ambitions, was brought about by a serious verdict on her state of health. The illness (asthma) that she had lived with since childhood was preparing its final outcome with increasing efficiency. The fact she lived in Paris, after Aix-en-Provence, in the terribly polluted air of a capital that was so welcoming to cars, could only have intensified her worry. On 30 August, she noted in her *Journal*: 'Perhaps not so much time left.' And a little later (10 September) she wrote down this sentence that Boswell attributes to the famous Dr Johnson: 'When a man knows he is to be hanged in an hour… it concentrates his mind wonderfully.'

The second decision involved a review of how she conceived of what she called, in the *Journal*, 'the photographer's task'. The following extracts illustrate this point.

II

Extracts from Alix's *Journal*, 1979*

The act of developing and printing. Bringing out of the dark, into the light. An act of recollection. Through memory, we can continue to 'touch' the piece of the world captured in a photograph (*30 August*).

The effort to hold a piece of the world in its instant, the 'encounter with Uncle Émile and the Eiffel Tower', this is the photographer's task (*2 September*).

A photograph worthy of the name does not give you a view of the world, it lets you touch it (*5 September*).

To what extent is what 'comes out of the dark', born of 'nothing', consistent with the memory of the picture taken. Because the photographer didn't just <u>see</u> the world, he encountered it more or less simultaneously with his other senses at the same time; he heard it, breathed, tasted, touched it even (*10 September*).

In July, a memory of Athens. Very vivid: the water, the sun, an almost transparent pebble pulled from the water, I can feel it in my hand. I jotted it all down, I described I wrote. Today, I'm re-reading it. The memory is there. But is it? No. The image is duller. What with the sun, the pebble must have been covered in salt. And it's not my memory from July that I remember. <u>I'm remembering what I wrote.</u> Same thing with the negative (*15 September*).

Images, not *pictions* (Witt.) (*19 September*).

---

* These previously unseen extracts from the journal appear prior to the sections that have been published in Alix Cléo Roubaud – *Journal (1979-1983)* (Seuil, 1984, 2nd ed., 2009).

A negative is just a variety of colours (2 *October*).

I have a truly Berkeleyan mistrust of the negative (6 *October*).

So. The negative. Throw it away, really quickly. It's the only solution (7 *October*).

Destroying the negative will safeguard against the temptation to get close to the memory of the world contained in the photograph all over again. Once the print has been made, this memory is lost, or more precisely, is just a memory of the memory.
A negative is just a painter's palette (*11 October*).

The negative will be worked on in the darkroom for as long as there is something left of the memory of the whole experience to reproduce (*14 October*).

The negative should only be kept for as long as the result of processing it retains something of the living memory of the intended image (*17 October*).

I will only make a very small number of prints. Ideally, just one, if the process succeeds at the first attempt (*18 October*).

Supporting the resurrection of the image: that is the aim (*1 November*).

III

FEW OF ALIX'S photographs were shown in public during her lifetime. She occasionally displayed some pictures privately, in her workshop on rue Vieille-du-Temple, for a few friends. Reactions to her work varied. She noted this, at times, in the *Journal*, with a degree of self-irony. The only meaningful recognition she received, the exhibition of her series *Si quelque chose noir* at the Rencontres photographiques d'Arles in 1983, was posthumous. And then the prints were not hers. Perhaps she would not have chosen to show them in the same format.

Until very recently, it was only possible to get an idea of her work from a handful of reproductions that appear in the *Journal*. Even though their number was increased for the second edition, they only represent a very limited number of pictures. At best, they are illustrations that accompany the text of the *Journal*.

'I began my work at the start of 2008,' writes Hélène Giannecchini. She was given access to all the prints I had kept, which were waiting, quite precariously, on top of a wardrobe.

There was a perfectly feasible way of approaching these items: by considering that this previously unseen bundle was composed of a whole heap of documents that might shed light on the *Journal*, in greater depth than the 'illustrations' featuring in it had done, and on an important period in the life of its author. This research would eventually lead to a biography. If this option was chosen, the 600-odd prints that had been kept, along with the biographical information gathered from witness interviews, would form the starting point for a critical study of the *Journal*, which is a prose work. It is as a work of prose rather than an autobiographical document that the *Journal* has been received, occasionally commented on, and generally linked to the book of poetry that I published in 1986, *Quelque chose noir*, which very clearly responds to and dialogues with it.

This was not Hélène Giannecchini's approach from the outset. That is, she did not take the *Journal* as her point of departure, to examine how the photographic archive, the 'collection of documents', illuminates it, but on the contrary, focused on the body of photographic work. She explains it very clearly here: 'Alix is often just the dead wife of a [...] writer, her marriage thus eclipsing her work. At best, she is the muse for whom he erected a tomb in his poetry collection *Quelque chose noir.*' She set out to reverse 'the concept of muse that artistic tradition is so attached to. There is a temptation to read Alix's work as completely autobiographical. It isn't. Her work was rooted in lived experience – a common practice – but she managed to extricate herself from those extreme states to offer something else.'

Hélène Giannecchini's book represents a stage in this research. It is not only the result of her careful examination of the prints, the considerable work she put into sorting and classifying the photographs, the cataloguing, and her preparation of the bequests that were made to various institutions (Centre Pompidou, Maison européenne de la photographie, Bibliothèque nationale de France, Musée des beaux-arts de Montréal, Médiathèque de Lyon, IMEC and others), but it also emphasizes the self-professed theoretical background of the body of work (which you might oversimplify as being Wittgenstein-Steinian), bringing to light Alix's conception of the art of photography and the particular way in which she intended to inscribe herself in its history.

This book doesn't pass over the autobiographical dimension of Alix Cléo Roubaud's work, but it puts its importance into perspective. The chapter that Hélène Giannecchini dedicates to a detailed study of one of the photographs in the collection, *Quinze minutes la nuit au rythme de la respiration*, is, I believe, the most accomplished example of the depth of her approach.

*

Here is what I wrote in 1985, in response to the photograph commented on by Hélène Giannecchini on p. 111.[18]

ON MY TABLE, to the left of the typewriter, is a photograph in the fringes of the lamplight, which casts a shadow (that of the left side of the typewriter) over the right margin of the picture, bathing the rest as it sits, motionless, among the rubber, pencil sharpener, two Kleenex, crumpled bits of paper covered in pencil, a collection of felt-tip pens in four colours, and the typescript of the 'great fire of London' in its orange-yellow folders; it is a page-sized image, in landscape orientation, slightly larger than the format of the *Journal*, the book comprising a selection of Alix's typed and handwritten meditations, where the picture appears, in smaller scale, on p. 91:

> To photograph the familiar – ... – the extraordinary, the strange – and even more so where the two come together.

The black and white photograph, the only one for me, resembles a page and ink, with its signs borrowed from the light. Today my lamp places it in a dark margin where it glows in all its blackness, the dominant black that extends through the image. A large black mass covers more than half of it, at first appearing uniform (from a glance snatched between the boundaries of the lamplight and the darkness) but then separating into two areas, both black, but one of which – the bottom one, at the picture's bottom edge – is less dense, not as absolute; the separation of these two intensities of black creates an angle, with the lower section appearing horizontal and the upper one vertical, a wall of darkness rising above the ground's surface, which is also dark and black, but a little less so.

Towards the top, the mass of vertical black strokes is in turn divided, distinctly this time, prominently even, torn into peaks cleaved by gulfs of light: very steep mountains, several heights of mountains sinking into the background of the image, a depth implied by the fading of blacks into greys; mountains observed from the floor of a dark valley, dark with the great wall of black that rises vertically in front of it; a dark valley without detail, hardly touched, only minimally, by a few photons fallen from the colourless sky; mountains sinking into other mountains, grey ones, lit from very far away.

These would be mountains except the air above them is also invaded by black: a black this time like smoke; the mountains are not solid, deep, but made of thick smoke, black with a smoke whose flames cannot be seen, or rather whose flames are black too, are the smoke itself; a black fire; a smoke-fire made up of one black colour; a dark fire which reflects the light that reveals it, shapes it, infuses it from behind with grey and dispels it into wisps of smoke.

These are not mountains, they are flames leaning leftwards, obscure flames that do not reach upwards towards the sky but bend beneath the light visible on the right, the faraway light that envelops them with its brightness, defines them as flames; the flames bend under the light, and under the invisible wind too, which blows from the illuminated corner, on the right, where the gulf of light is deepest; the wind and the light come from there, as the photograph shows in its pure naivety (not the naivety of the photographer, but the distinct, innate simplicity of this art form, which plays at truth): 'the familiar, the strange, where the two come together.'

Each wick, plume, with a visible flame is doubled; each candle of flames has its grey double behind it; its grey halo, its grey portrait drawn in light, which seems to have been captured several times over, marking a hesitation.

THIS IS A MOONLESS NIGHT, though there are stars: the stars give off their light, but their effect on the photographic salts is slow, as though the extreme distance were indicated less by the faintness of the trace left than by its slowness, its reluctance to make an impression on the minutely thin surface.

The photograph is not of flames, even black ones, not of mountains swallowed by the dark night, but of cypresses; cypresses at night, black candles moved by the wind, smoke-flames. Sitting on the warm stone, in the nocturnal October wind, with my legs against the dry-stone wall, I am reminded of the heat of the same stone in August, the sumptuous early days of August 1980: the air filled with stars, the vines, the olive trees drawn in black and dusty white, a breathing night, fragrant in the heat. That moonless night under the stars, on the warm stone, Alix came up with the idea of photographing the night, capturing the weight of this slowness, this ancient light from the farthest reaches, on the black and white page; it is a photograph of a naked night, and a photograph taken when naked at night, with the camera held against her unclothed chest, directly against her chest, naked. It is natural to look towards these trees, taking them in, rather than looking into the distance, Conques, the Montagne Noire, the slope of olive trees, the azaroles, the pines entangled with broom shrubs.

The alley of cypresses comes up to this point, to the large flat stones, and that night, the hot night in August that I am talking about, the two ascending lines were emphatically black, under the gaze of the stars' tiny pinpricks, but were beyond touch, impermeable, impenetrable.

Each cypress tree is shaped like a flame, and has a black body even in daytime, radiates inwardly in daylight, like a flame, which is also absorbed into itself, pulled towards the devouring of air within. The cypresses reach up towards the sky like columns of black, burning air. The cypresses in the alley each remained visible in the procession climbing up towards us on the hill, visible and each one separate in its exquisite darkness, defying perception by an unwavering gaze. From the highest, lightest spot at the top of the hill, it seemed like it would be impossible to show them. There was nothing hostile about them, nor were they distanced by solitude or silence, or some inability to distinguish them. But their double-file, countable sequence resisted measurement through a *depiction*.

And immediately desire, unthought like all desire, arose from this resistance opposed not to seeing, but to the intention to offer, to the seeing eye, this flat and identically reproducible memory, a photograph. This also meant an impulse to identify with an autonomous element, a sympathy with the shape, its straight, stubborn ascent.

BUT THE CYPRESS TREES were not moving then: at the time I remember, the time of my writing, October, there was a mild Cers wind wrapping itself round my legs, which stubbornly lashed the hill that rises above the dry-stone wall, and the cypress trees leaned, not towards the left in a breeze coming from the other direction but forward; they bowed their heads like they always do, like flames, like candles at night in a bedroom with the windows open, like mountains heavy with night when you look at them intently. In October of that earlier year, in the mild Cers of two o'clock in the morning, I remembered, as I remember now, the photograph entitled *Quinze minutes la nuit au rythme de la respiration* (the two memories overlap, become indistinct; I remember now, looking at the image, and I remember remembering), that moment in August, also at night; the cypress trees were not moving then. And Alix, standing up, looking at the alley of cypress trees, the air was hot, still, peaceful in the darkness, there was no wind.

If, in the photograph, the flames of the black cypresses lean, like wisps of smoke, towards the left, it is not some past August wind weighing on the trees whose effects are shown in the picture, which is motionless, suspending the view and light, but the movements of the camera that Alix had placed against her breasts, naked, against the heat; the leaning is imposed by the direction of the camera's mechanical gaze.

> Taken at night with an exposure of 10-15 minutes. Slight motion up and down [...] due to my breathing.

The motion caused by her breathing sends the cypresses up in smoke towards the top; towards the top and side. The cypresses on the left of the picture are swept upwards towards the sky in black and grey smoke, not from the 'pneumatic' effect of the Cers but due to her breathing, which lifts her breasts and the camera. The picture inherits her breath. That is why this photograph is as much a photograph of her breathing as it is one of the cypresses: attention to her breath, to the rhythm and motion of her respiration which infuses the inert, motionless image of the alley of cypress trees indirectly, capturing the pinprick light of the stars over the time of the image's exposure.

This photograph is an impassioned and unhappy homage to respiration, to breath, which its author, who had been asthmatic since childhood (she would later die because of the illness), found a way to etch into the image, to trace in the ink of these black candles whose outlines, so distinct, so autonomous in the dark night, dissipated into the air, leaving a mist on the glass covering the picture. The indirect effect of her breathing deprived the cypress-forms of their sharpness, their identity even, from a distance.

This is an image of loving and struggling for air, of the impossible passion for breath of someone ailed by air; and the alley of cypresses, with its tranquillity, its dark ascent, and its history, was a perfect metonym for this family home where a person afflicted with asthma cannot be without suffering, without suffocating.

THEA PETROU

Chère Hélène...

WHEN I FIRST READ *Une image peut-être vraie* in 2014, I was a student, in Paris researching Jacques Roubaud's poetry – his love poetry. One of the collections I was looking at was *Quelque chose noir*, which was written in the wake of Alix Cléo Roubaud's death. Strictly speaking, it was not written exactly in the wake of her death. For almost 30 months Jacques Roubaud did not write any poetry at all, finding the lyrical too painful now that the first reader – listener – of his poetry, the addressee of his poems, was gone. Emerging from this grieving silence, *Quelque chose noir* attempts a tentative dialogue with Alix Cléo Roubaud, responding to thoughts she had confided in her journal, and expressing an empathy with her respiratory difficulties through the irregular spacing of the words on the page.

It was on reading *Quelque chose noir* that you decided to set off in search of Alix Cléo Roubaud:

> I began my work on Alix Cléo Roubaud at the start of 2008. It was on reading *Quelque chose noir*, the volume of elegiac poetry dedicated to her by Jacques Roubaud, that I wanted to fill in the interstices where I thought I imagined her. I realized, after getting caught up in her life and her work, that the interest of the archive does not lie

so much in the result itself as in the approach: complete immersion in a life which is not mine, carrying out an investigation with no resolution.

Looking for her voice, wanting to imagine her side of the dialogue, even if you knew it would be impossible to find.

Yours was the first writing I had read that put Alix Cléo Roubaud and her work at the front and centre of its intention. It is still, today, the only book-length work to approach her photography from the multiple facets that you do. 'And just as Alix appeared to me in fragments, letters, images, and through reconstructed accounts, so too I wish to write.' Fragments, you have called them, scattered shards that nonetheless form the most detailed, sensitive and considered portrait of the artist that we have.

Yours was the only writing to ask whether Alix Cléo Roubaud was not more than her marriage to a great writer, whether the years outside their relationship – the years not selected for inclusion in the published version of her *Journal* – did not count, 'everything is reduced to their story'.

Yours was the first book I read that I wanted to translate, the reason I became a translator.

As a student looking for ways to prove a hypothesis, and often reminded by my supervisors of the need to better 'signpost' my writing, I was moved by your admission that you wanted to work in the interstices, by your proposal of the fragment as the most honest form for the material you had gathered. As an academic trained in objectivity and passive voice(s), I admired you when you wrote that you preferred the first-person narrative pronoun 'I' to all other voices, its 'modesty', its honesty, the promise of ignorance that comes with its subjectivity forming a level of protection against an insistence that your subject 'was this or that'.

As a translator, I slipped comfortably into your 'I' and felt at ease in your voice. Perhaps because I felt an affinity between the work of the translator and that of the archivist-curator, between the whittling down of a translation from its plump, lumpy rough draft to its sleeker final version and the building of an archive, with all the circumscribing – what constitutes evidence of a life? – that it involves. When you described the process of cataloguing a photograph so it becomes a searchable object in a museum or library collection, you mentioned the 'space' that persists between one choice of subject search term and another, leaving the trace of the unknown cataloguer forever in the record. And this reminded me of translating, the indecision over which word to choose to fit meaning, context and register, which definition to prioritize in a list of multiple possibilities. It comes down to fear and shame, I think. At speaking out of turn on behalf of our subjects, saying too much in their voices. Leaving our trace in a story that does not belong to us, entirely.

And perhaps I can confess, here in this letter, that this feeling was intensified when it came to translating the excerpts of Alix Cléo Roubaud's writing that you interwove with your account of her life and work, passages from letters she had written, the notebooks she had kept that constituted her journal, and other texts: stories, conceptual descriptions of photography, scripts documenting telephone exchanges with close friend Jean Eustache. Her particular use of grammar, vocabulary and punctuation, and her sometimes elliptical phrasing, often left me with more 'space' than I would have wished for as her translator. You have said you would struggle to recognize Alix Cléo Roubaud's singular intonation were you to hear her voice somewhere other than in the film recording of *Les Photos d'Alix*, through too little personal experience of it. I have sometimes felt reluctant to let go of a section of her text, to allow meaning to settle and be still. Wanting to fill in the interstices where I think I imagine a person.

Alix Cléo Roubaud's journal reflected her bilingualism, with passages written in English as well as French. As I made my way through your book, writing the first draft of my translation, I did not stop to check which of the journal entries (all in French in your work) had originally been written in English. These are two extracts I first translated into my own English, before going back to the *Journal* and finding them in Alix Cléo Roubaud's English:

> *Je suis un ratage complet pas une photographie même les livres me terrifient lire les romans policiers les plus bêtes me plonge dans la panique ivre la nuit*
>
> TP: I am a complete failure not one photograph even books terrify me reading the silliest detective novels sends me into a panic drunk at night
>
> ACR: I am a complete fraud not a photograph even books terrify me reading the silliest detective novels drives me into a panic drunk at night
>
> *Terrifiée à l'idée de recommencer ô c'était ô si facile avec toi tout près*
>
> TP: Terrified at the thought of starting over o it was o so easy with you close by
>
> ACR: terrified of beginning the agony all over o it was o so easy with you here

In both cases, I noted that my translation was a little less specific, a little less distinct, compared to what Alix Cléo Roubaud had originally written. I too had not picked up the particular inflection of her voice.

One of the most pleasurable aspects of translating *Une image peut-être vraie* has been navigating Alix Cléo Roubaud's photographs and her darkroom more closely than I had as a reader. I had been guilty of looking to her pictures to validate my reading, not only of the *Journal* but also of Jacques Roubaud's writing, his projection, in poetry, of memories as images and photographs. Holding up the images to the text as proof of a theory. 'Recognition brings a certain pleasure, but it is not seeing.'

You have sometimes used the expression 'faire une photographie' in the book. The verb *faire* – make or do in English – can replace *prendre* – take – without it conferring the sense of creating, crafting or manufacturing that *making* does in English. But when you have written 'faire une photographie' in descriptions of Alix Cléo Roubaud's photography practice, I have understood and translated it as a reference to her making rather than taking a photograph.

When Alix recreates a childhood memory of sitting in the back of a car, with her view of her father limited to the back of his head and shoulders, and the features contained in the rear-view mirror – his eyes, encircled again by the dark rims of his glasses – she uses double exposure to introduce the ghostly mirage of her mother into the image, layering her face over the original picture of her father. The original photograph, the one just of her father, is a familiar memory to me. I remember this view of my own father, driving me to school or on family trips, the back of his head partially obstructed by the headrest of the driver's seat, and his big hands on the wheel. When the spectral apparition of Alix's mother looks back at me from the picture, I'm reminded that this is not my memory, and that the particular subjectivity of memory is the most devastating of all, fading inexorably into oblivion when a person dies. I think of you, Hélène, collecting shopping lists and medication wrappers that had been slipped into Alix's books as page markers, attempting to rescue these traces of memory, while knowing they had no place in the archive and your research, traces which must have seemed so precious, so personal, because you'd never had the chance to meet her.

In other photographs, Alix intervenes in the frame, again after the shot has been taken, by hand-etching in waves and lines using the thin beam of a torch – her *pinceau lumineux* – a brush that produces black paint from light. From your alignment of photography with painting, particularly the Abstract Expressionism that influenced Alix's approach in the darkroom, I see the way she took possession of her prints, allowing her emotion and state of mind to infiltrate the image through the spontaneous movements of her hands. You have described the 'fiction' of these photographs, the elements not captured through the viewfinder, and I realize that the darkroom was a place for escape and invention, but also a place where fear and pain would sometimes rise to the surface.

In her best-known series, *Si quelque chose noir,* Alix invests her body in the photographs, allowing her movements around the room – her brother-in-law's workshop in Saint-Félix – to be imprinted on the film over a long exposure time. A ballet of sorts, but also a battle of a person against her demons, the taming of a beast. You explored the many faces of the beast: depression, the craft of photography, death. And looking back at the photographs after translating your commentary of Alix's battle, I'm struck by the strange sense of vitality that I now see in the sequence (which is nonetheless a sequence of stills): the excess of light streaming in through the window, the laughing child who looks on over her fate, the multiple figures of Alix as she descends into her grave. I first came across the title of Alix's series through Jacques Roubaud's *Quelque chose noir,* in which that indeterminable 'some thing' paints his life black after Alix's death. In Alix's sequence, I can now see the hypothetical 'If' of *Si quelque chose noir,* the impossible possibility – in the photographs – that the outcome will somehow be different.

In *Le Baiser,* a play on perspective is activated by the loosening or tightening of the framing. As with other, more explicitly, erotic photographs, Alix stages the shot, choreographing bodies within and beyond the viewfinder, herself too slipping into and out of the frame. The viewer is alternately voyeur and watched interloper, Alix's careful arrangement of her subjects establishing an intricate network of desire that extends from the photograph to whomever is looking at it. When I first saw the intimate photographs of Alix and Jacques Roubaud in your book, and at the retrospective you curated in Paris, I was looking for the poet and his muse, for clues that would unlock the secrets in his poetry. I didn't see myself in the network of gazes until you pointed out the hidden eye watching me back, warning me that things are not what they seem, not always what we expect them to be. I felt self-conscious as viewer-voyeur, but I wonder if I will always search these images for clues. Even as I see you see me. Even as I see myself.

Rooted in my heart, like the evergreen cypress trees in Saint-Félix – 'unlikely to fall in my lifetime' – is your fragment on 'Breathing'. Here an X-ray of Alix's respiratory system is the subject of the image, its form – the shifting relationship of black, white and grey – inscribed in the photograph by the motion of her breathing as the camera rises and falls against her chest over a 15-minute exposure. This was the first section of the book that I translated, and the last stop on your route through the places where Alix had existed. I thought it stood alone and told a story. About illness and the desire to live, about your search. What do we think we will find – what do we need to find – when we go looking for the *that-has-been* of a photograph? 'I was able to calm an unchecked mysticism that had been troubling me.'

Making then, not taking. Through your wandering into the lexical fields of memory, action painting, dance, bullfighting, medicine and eroticism, I have followed Alix's processes in the darkroom and observed the imposition of her own physicality – a performance – on the film. And now I see the pictures, what they are made of.

Thank you, Hélène.

List of Photographs and Illustrations

All photographs are gelatin-silver prints by Alix Cléo Roubaud.

p. 17   Alix Cléo Roubaud on a beach in Greece, May 1967, Alix Cléo Roubaud collection.

p. 28   *Sans titre*, portrait of Marc Blanchette, circa 1980, Bibliothèque nationale de France.

p. 37   *Sans titre* (self-portrait with *pinceau lumineux*), circa 1979, Montfort-l'Amaury, private collection.

p. 40   *Sans titre*, from series *Alcools, hommage à Morris Louis*, December 1980, Centre Georges-Pompidou, MNAM-CCI/DIST. RMN-GP, ©Alix Cléo Roubaud/Guy Carrard.

p. 41   *Sans titre*, from series *Alcools, hommage à Morris Louis*, December 1980, private collection.

p. 45   *Sans titre* (portrait of Arthur Edward Blanchette), circa 1980, private collection.

p. 47   *Sans titre* (double exposure showing Marcelle Blanchette's face superimposed on portrait of Arthur Edward Blanchette), circa 1980, private collection.

p. 52   *Tombe de Ludwig Witgenstein*, Cambridge, 1980, private collection.

p. 56   Handwritten letter from Jean Eustache to Alix Cléo Roubaud, circa 1980, Alix Cléo Roubaud collection.

p. 58   Handwritten postcard from Jean Eustache to Alix Cléo Roubaud, with *Massacre of the Innocents* by Pierre Bruegel on the reverse (Kunsthistorisches Museum, Vienna), 1979, Alix Cléo Roubaud collection.

p. 60   Jean Eustache, Alix Cléo Roubaud and Boris Eustache on the film set of *Les photos d'Alix*, 1980, private collection.

p. 63   *Sans titre* (portrait of Jean Eustache), 1980, Bibliothèque nationale de France.

p. 66   *Sans titre* (portrait of Jean Eustache), 1980, Bibliothèque nationale de France.

p. 67   *Sans titre* (portrait of Jean Eustache), detail from a contact sheet, 1981, Alix Cléo Roubaud collection.

p. 68   *Sans titre* (portrait of Jean Eustache), 1980, private collection.

p. 74   *Sans titre*, from series *La Dernière Chambre*, 1980, private collection.

p. 82   *Deux soeurs qui ne sont pas soeurs*, circa 1980, private collection.

p. 84   *Sans titre*, from series *Correction de perspective dans ma chambre*, circa 1980-1981, private collection.

p. 85   *Sans titre*, from series *Correction de perspective dans ma chambre*, circa 1980-1981, private collection.

p. 90   *Sans titre* (Alix Cléo and Jacques Roubaud), circa 1980, Bibliothèque municipale de Lyon.

p. 91   *Sans titre* (Alix Cléo and Jacques Roubaud), circa 1980, Maison européenne de la photographie.

p. 92   *Le 31.v.80, University Arms Hotel, Cambridge (ch. 217)*, Centre Georges-Pompidou, MNAM-CCI/DIST. RMN-GP ©Alix Cléo Roubaud/Guy Carrard.

p. 94   *Sans titre*, contact sheet, 1979, Alix Cléo Roubaud collection.

p. 98   *Sans titre* (Jacques and Alix Cléo Roubaud on the left, Alix Cléo Roubaud on the right), detail from a contact sheet, 1980, Alix Cléo Roubaud collection.

p. 99   *Sans titre* (Alix Cléo and Jacques Roubaud), 1980, Maison européenne de la photographie.

p. 99   VIII.*80 Saint-Félix* (Alix Cléo and Jacques Roubaud), 1980, Bibliothèque nationale de France.

p. 100 *Le 14.v.80., Hôtel de France, ch. 15, Avignon* (Alix Cléo and Jacques Roubaud), 1980, Maison européenne de la photographie.

p. 100   *Sans titre* (handwritten texts by Jacques Roubaud), detail from a contact sheet, 1979, Alix Cléo Roubaud collection.

p. 102   *Vertigo le 14.VII.79 – le 14.XII.79*, Bibliothèque municipale de Lyon.

p. 110   *Sans titre* (view of the main hall in the Grands Thermes de La Bourboule), 1980, Institut Mémoires de l'édition contemporaine.

p. 111   *Quinze minutes la nuit au rythme de la respiration*, 1980, Centre Georges-Pompidou, MNAM-CCI/DIST. RMN-GP ©Alix Cléo Roubaud/Guy Carrard.

p. 113   X-ray image of Alix Cléo Roubaud's lungs carried out by Aix-en-Provence angiology clinic, 29 January 1975, Alix Cléo Roubaud collection.

p. 116   *Les Carnets, le 5 août 1980 la Tuilerie de St-Félix* (Alix Cléo and Jacques Roubaud), Bibliothèque municipale de Lyon.

p. 122   Slides of series *Si quelque chose noir*, 1980-1981, Alix Cléo Roubaud collection.

p. 125   *Si quelque chose noir 8/17*, 1980-1981, Bibliothèque nationale de France.

p. 127   *Si quelque chose noir 5/17*, 1980-1981, Bibliothèque nationale de France.

p. 129   *Si quelque chose noir 16/17*, 1980-1981, Bibliothèque nationale de France.

p. 130   *Si quelque chose noir 12/17*, 1980-1981, Bibliothèque nationale de France.

p. 131   *Si quelque chose noir 14/17*, 1980-1981, Bibliothèque nationale de France.

p. 133   Trial for *Si quelque chose noir*, 1980-1981, Institut Mémoires de l'Édition contemporaine.

p. 134   *Si quelque chose noir*, introductory text, 1980-1981, Bibliothèque nationale de France.

p. 135   Alix Cléo Roubaud at *Une autre photographie* exhibition (10 January–30 March 1982), Maison des arts André-Malraux, 1982, Institut Mémoires de l'édition contemporaine.

p. 138   Front: *La Cuillère*, Saint-Félix, 1980. Reverse: invitation handwritten by Alix Cléo Roubaud addressed to Martine Broda, Wednesday 4 March 1981, not sent, Alix Cléo Roubaud collection.

p. 141   *Sans titre* (remake of a photograph of Auguste Renoir and Stéphane Mallarmé taken by Edgar Degas), circa 1980, Bibliothèque nationale de France.

p. 151   *Sans titre* (Alix Cléo and Jacques Roubaud), detail from a contact sheet, Saint-Félix, 1980, Alix Cléo Roubaud collection.

p. 152   Fig. 1: *Le Baiser*, Saint-Félix, 1980, Bibliothèque nationale de France.

p. 153   Fig. 2: *Le Baiser*, Saint-Félix, 1980, Bibliothèque nationale de France.

p. 155   Fig. 3: *Le Baiser*, Saint-Félix, 1980, private collection.

p. 157   *Si quelque chose noir 17/17*, Saint-Félix, 1980, Bibliothèque nationale de France.

p. 159   *Chiswick*, 1980, private collection.

Endnotes

1. Georges Perec, 'Texte lu aux noces d'Alix-Cléo Blanchette et de Jacques Roubaud', in *Beaux presents belles absentes* (Paris: Seuil, 1994), pp. 61-62.
2. Alix Cléo Roubaud, *Letters to Sylvie*, October 1968, Alix Cléo Roubaud collection.
3. Ludwig Wittgenstein, *Culture and Value*, ed. by G. H. von Wright, trans. by Peter Winch, Oxford, Blackwell Publishing, 1998, p. 36e.
4. Alix Cléo Roubaud, *Script written for Jean Eustache*, Alix Cléo Roubaud collection, 1979.
5. Alix Cléo Roubaud, *preparatory notes for 'On Les Photos d'Alix'*, Alix Cléo Roubaud collection, January 1981.
6. Alix Cléo Roubaud, *Script written for Jean Eustache*, Alix Cléo Roubaud collection, 1979.
7. Gertrude Stein, *The Geographical History of America*, New York, Random House, 1937; new ed. Baltimore, Johns Hopkins University Press, 1995.
8. Alix Cléo Roubaud, *Research Notebook*, February 1980, Alix Cléo Roubaud collection.
9. Michel Serres, *Hermes III, la traduction*, Paris, Éditions de Minuit, 1974.
10. *Colloque sur la traduction poétique. Centre Afrique-Asie-Europe de la Sorbonne nouvelle*, Afterword by Roger Caillois, Paris, Gallimard, 1978.
11. Elizabeth Bishop, *Géographie III*, trans. by Alix Cléo Roubaud, Linda Orr and Claude Mouchard, Paris, Circé, 1991.
12. *Lifting Belly: An Erotic Poem by Gertrude Stein,* Counterpoint, Berkeley, California, first Counterpoint edition 2020, pp. 21-22.
13. Alix Cléo Roubaud, *Journal*, op. cit., p. 233.
14. Alix Cléo Roubaud, Letter to her family, La Bourboule, August 1978, Alix Cléo Roubaud collection.
15. Letter to her family, Alix Cléo Roubaud collection, 1980.
16. *Journal*, op. cit, p. 201.
17. Alix Cléo Roubaud, Letter to her family dated 31 December 1979, Alix Cléo Roubaud collection.
18. Jacques Roubaud, *Le Grand Incendie de Londres*, Paris, Seuil, 1989, p. 393ff.

Alix's Cléo Roubaud's Works

Alcools, hommage à Morris Louis	Alcohol, Homage to Morris Louis
Le Baiser	The Kiss
Les Carnets	The Notebooks
Correction de perspective dans ma chambre	Correction of Perspective in my Bedroom
La Cuillère	The Spoon
La Dernière chambre	The Last Bedroom
Deux sœurs qui ne sont pas sœurs	Two Sisters Who Are Not Sisters
Quinze minutes la nuit au rythme de la respiration	Fifteen Minutes at Night to the Rhythm of Breathing
Sans titre	Untitled
Si quelque chose noir	If Some Thing Black
Tombe de Ludwig Wittgenstein	Grave of Ludwig Wittgenstein

Note to the Reader

The collection that nurtures this work was entrusted to me by Jacques Roubaud. The documents (letters, photographs, texts, among others) were produced during their time together, from December 1979 (when they first met) until Alix Cléo Roubaud's death in January 1983.
Documents from before this period are rare.

The passages cited are extracts from the *Journal* of Alix Cléo Roubaud (Éditions du Seuil, 'Fiction & Cie', 1984) in the second edition published in 2009, exact retranscriptions of documents belonging to the Alix Cléo Roubaud collection (letters, notebooks, essays, for example), or excerpts from interviews that I was able to conduct with those who knew her.

Acknowledgements

HÉLÈNE GIANNECCHINI would like to thank:

Jacques Roubaud for his trust and confidence. He gave me access to unseen documents and pictures that have formed the basis of this book.

Clement Chéroux, Anne Biroleau, Françoise Lonardoni and Martine Dionne for their support and for their part in enabling the recognition of Alix's work; as well as Jean-Luc Monterosso and Stéphane Aquin for their interest.

Pierre, Denise and Anne Getzler for their warm welcome and generosity.

Marc, Militza, Viviane and Daniel Blanchette for letting me into Alix's apartment and entrusting me with their memories.

Dian Turnheim for her kindness, Anne McCauley and François Béguin for the interviews they granted me.

Astrid J. and Nina L. for their close readings.

Anne-Marie, Jean-François, Fleu, Mathieu and Anne for being there.

Maurice Olender who had the faith to encourage me to write this book.

SYLPH EDITIONS would like to thank Thea Petrou for initiating this translation and for her wholehearted dedication to this project from gestation to publication.

About the Author

HÉLÈNE GIANNECCHINI is a writer and art theorist. She has a doctorate in literature and specializes in the relationship between text and image. She writes books, organizes exhibitions and works with contemporary artists.

She is the author of *Une Image peut-être vraie* (2014) and *Voir de ses propres yeux* (2020), both published by Éditions du Seuil. Her next book, *Un Désir démesuré d'amitié*, is due to be released by Seuil in September 2024. Her current research focuses on 20th-century LGBTQIA+ archives and narratives.

She held residencies at the Villa Medici, Rome (2018) and Villa Albertine, New York (2022).

Colophon

First published in 2014 by Éditions du Seuil in French as *Une image peut-être vraie. Alix Cléo Roubaud*.

©Éditions du Seuil, 2014
Images: ©Hélène Giannecchini, Jacques Roubaud
Translation: ©Thea Petrou, 2024

No part of this publication may be reproduced in any form whatsoever without the prior written permission of the publisher.

Editorial of the translation: Mona Gainer-Salim
Design: Ornan Rotem
    Set in Sabon designed by Jan Tschichold, a classic modern typeface based on 16th-century models

Printed by TJ Books Ltd, Padstow

SYLPH EDITIONS · London · 2024
ISBN 978-1-909631-44-1
www.sylpheditions.com